C
o o

20

BY THE LABOUR OF THEIR HANDS

The Story of
Ontario Cheddar Cheese

Quarry Press

HERITAGE

Rivers of Oil: *The Founding of North America's Petroleum Industry*
Hope Morritt

Sir John A. Macdonald: *The Man and the Politician*
Donald Swainson

Sir Wilfred Laurier: *The Great Conciliator*
Barbara Robertson

Finnigan's Guide to the Ottawa Valley: *A Cultural and Historical Companion*
Joan Finnigan

Brado's Guide to Ottawa: *A Cultural and Historical Companion*
Edward Brado

Bowering's Guide To Eastern Ontario: *A Cultural and Historical Companion*
Ian Bowering

Fitsell's Guide to the Old Ontario Strand: *A Cultural and Historical Companion*
Bill Fitsell and **Michael Dawber**

Old Scores, New Goals: *The Story of the Ottawa Senators*
Joan Finnigan

BY THE LABOUR OF THEIR HANDS

The Story of Ontario Cheddar Cheese

by
Heather Menzies

QUARRY PRESS

The publication of this book is generously supported by the Ontario Heritage Foundation.

The publisher gratefully acknowledges the support of The Canada Council, the Ontario Arts Council, the Department of Canadian Heritage, and the Ontario Publishing Centre.

Canadian Cataloguing in Publication Data

Menzies, Heather, 1949–
    By the labour of their hands: the story of Ontario
cheddar cheese:

ISBN 1-55082-102-4

    1. Cheese industry — Ontario — History.
I. Title

HD9280.C3306 1994   338.1′773′0971309
C94-900283-6

Design by Susan Hannah.

Printed and bound in Canada by Webcom Limited, Toronto, Ontario.

Published by Quarry Press Inc., P.O. Box 1061, Kingston, Ontario.

CONTENTS

❦

For my father
DONALD C. MENZIES (1916–1984)
corporate manager and hobby farmer . . .

and for my great-uncle
DONALD MENZIES (1879–1965)
Molesworth cheesemaker and
government cheese grader . . .

Foreword

Molesworth Cheese & Butter Factory

Molesworth
Cheese and Butter Factory

Summers for me smelled like the Graham Creamery and Fraser's Cheese House. The former was warm and wet, cement floors slicked down with hoses. Sweet-smelling whey dripped from freshly packed presses along one wall. The creamery was a bright, echoey place filled with shiny stainless steel. Up the road past McCrimmon's Corners, John Fraser's cheese-curing warehouse was dark; its creaking pine floors were thick with muffling sawdust. The dim recesses in the back were filled with rows of shelves, each one filled with 90-pound rounds of cheese. Their smooth, yellow-white curves glimmered softly in the light from the dusty, 40-watt bulbs hanging between the rows. The air was cool and pungent with wood chips and the fierce, almost acrid, smell of aging Ontario cheddar.

As a child, I loved going into these places. Each was a complete little world sealed in with its aromas and a seemingly unique class of people — old people by and large, with a slow and rhythmic way of talking. Like my brothers and sister, I was looking for a bit of curd or a slice of Fraser's 10-year old "Cheddar Nip," the sharp taste of which shot up the back of my throat like a flame so strong it brought tears to my eyes. But I also noticed my father. My father seemed to change when he took us on these outings. Normally he was in a hurry, always with errands

to run, lists and lists of things to buy and do for the abandoned farm he'd bought as the family's weekend retreat from the city. But he seemed to slow right down when we got into a cheese factory. He'd sample the cheeses, buy much more than we actually needed, lean on the counter and smile as though he had all the time in the world for the stories Mr. Fraser and the others had to tell. He'd stay on and on, listening and smiling. It was as if he was honing in, sensing something strong and true behind the words and their cadence. They gave him a sense of well-being.

I'd guess now that it was the closest he got to going home. Raised in a family of farmers and cheesemakers rooted in an 1840s homestead at Molesworth in Western Ontario, my father ended up studying commerce at McGill. Then he went overseas during the war. Afterward, with shrapnel in his leg and his family gone, he settled into middle-management with a Montreal subsidiary of a British multinational. But on weekends and summer holidays, he took off his business suit and put away his horn-rimmed glasses. These were times for himself and for the farm he'd adopted in place of the original one at Molesworth. The one he bought was a derelict misfit from a by-gone era: it was set back from the road about a quarter mile, which was fine for sleighs but not for cars; the house had no toilet, running water, or central heating and was being gnawed away from the outside by a hundred brood mares which a neighbour pastured there for the summer. During the winter, he collected the urine in bags improvised out of old inner tubes and trucked the stuff to Montreal where an American pharmaceutical company extracted the hormone for women's face creams.

The horses had the run of the place while the last of the MacMillan family, who had homesteaded the land, lived out her declining years. After Miss MacMillan died, the pregnant horses stayed on, hungrily chewing the grass down into the ground, foraging on tree branches and gnawing windowsills for nourishment, while the farm sat unclaimed on the market — 200 acres of thin, worn-out soil.

On the high land, where the ground was most leeched and eroded, we planted trees, to put the land back to sleep, as I thought of it then. That done, we worked the fields. Weekend after weekend, we picked stones by hand, pulled weeds, then plowed and planted some hay. First we used a horse, borrowed from our neighbours, Archie and Enid Macdonald. The Macdonalds bred and trained carriage horses in the days before internal combustion; they too ran a brood-mare business. Later, with the help of other neighbours, the Bourciers, my father bid on a small tractor, and we began to seed some fields.

Except for the rushed weekends of tree-planting in the early spring, we children had to work only in the mornings. Afternoons, I would run with the dog, explore, and claim various spots as my own. One of these was a nearly limbless dead elm tree standing by itself on top of a slope we were gradually recovering in trees. Two stumpy branches remained, with the bulge where there'd been a third just visible between them. Frozen on the hill in pewtered stillness, it looked like a person with arms raised in prayer. To me, casting about among the trails gone cold from the people who'd been here before us, it seemed to represent these people: the MacMillans, and others I didn't know about. I visited the tree often, even talked to it, sensing or seeking through it some kind of continuity, a link to the land as it had been, even before it was cleared.

Odd artifacts, these: a dead old elm tree, the rhythm of old voices telling stories, and the smell of well-aged cheddar. But they guided me well in my journey back through time to better understand what I believe in now.

My generation, the post-war "baby boom," had a strangely a-historical sense of ourselves. It's not just that our parents grew up during the Depression and came of age during a six-year period of war and didn't much want to talk about these things. It was also because we were also the first generation of truly nuclear families,

Graham Creamery, Alexandria, Ontario, circa 1950.

raised in the suburbs. These were rigorously up-to-the-minute places, with street names like Elm, Maple, and Poplar, drawn from a hat and offering no clues about our place in time and social space. If we saw relatives from other generations, it was on pilgrimages so remote and rare that they were like visits to a zoo. My sole grandparent, my mother's father, was a pleasant old man who held a conch shell to his mouth and blew it like a horn. But I never knew why, nor how he'd learned this trick.

Instead, we got our stories from television. From that box in everyone's "family room," we also learned to cue ourselves through our peers. For many of us coming of age in the 1960s, this meant the student protest movement. At McGill University in the late '60s, I marched against the war in Vietnam and for French language rights in Quebec. I also joined the grape boycott and, later, the Kraft boycott, plus a sit-in for student representation in university administration and a teach-in on Canada's Indians.

It was not until I came to write this book that I realized the Kraft boycott was the closest of them all to being my own particular cause. It took all this time for me to understand also that the boycott was more than a refusal to buy Kraft cheese and peanut butter, although that's as far as most of us took it at the time. If anything, Kraft was a convenient scapegoat, deflecting us from what we had to grapple with if we really wanted to challenge what Kraft had come to represent. The real question is not so much how Kraft got so big and powerful. It is why Ontario cheddar got so small and weak that it couldn't defend itself and keep going.

In the late 1800s, cheddar cheese was second only to timber in export volume for Canada.[1] From the late 1800s into the early 1900s, when cheese was the staple source of protein in the diet of the English working class, eaten half a pound at a sitting in the noontime meal,[2] Canada (principally Ontario) supplied 70 per cent of Britain's huge import needs.[3] In the heyday of Ontario cheddar, there were 1,242 cheese factories dotted across the province, exporting over 200 million pounds of cheese a year.[4] Cheese accounted for 35 per cent of farmers' incomes.

Cheddar cheese wasn't just a business. For over a century, the cheddar cheese factory was the hub of the rural community and the heart of its rich oral culture. It was also one of its oldest hand crafts, bearing a tradition of creativity that dated back to the Middle Ages, before the separation of art from everyday life.

Traditional craft-scale cheddar cheese-making in Ontario declined for many understandable and unavoidable reasons; however, it needn't have shrunk to the struggling handful of small plants that exist today. It could have been preserved in a pluralistic mix of large and medium-scale cheese plants, some run according to global productivity standards and others according to craft and community priorities.

There was a time of reckoning in the late 1960s, when political leadership could have preserved the craft-scale cheddar cheese factories and honoured their traditions of craftsmanship in the continuity of Canadian history. Key politicians and bureaucrats were even advised on how this could be done.[5] But government and business leaders spurned the plan. Instead, they gave virtually exclusive priority to the interests of a group dominated by American dairy companies. My generation of well-meaning protesters contributed to the betrayal because we didn't know the story.

Canada is in a state of transition. The nation state is being replaced by larger, multinational units such as the European Economic Community and, here, what is shaping up to be a similar union scripted by the North American Free Trade Agreement. Canadians also have to choose between an increasingly homogenized North American or even world culture and a redefined Canadian society and culture that will preserve and nourish our distinctive traditions and values in a global political environment. But choosing the latter requires knowing what those values and traditions are, knowing our own stories and what they mean.

So this book looks at our past on two levels.

On a personal level, I'm continuing my quest for meaning among old artifacts. I'm following up on the sounds and smells of Ontario's traditional cheddar cheese factories, which anchored my father in a sense of place and time. On a more political level, I'm trying to discover why those factories have almost disappeared. I want to revisit the choices that were made along the way and to identify the values that were set aside in favour of the modern ones of efficiency and productivity.

Part I of the book sets the scene for the rise of Ontario cheddar. Part II is a personal journey of remembrance into the craft of Ontario cheddar and the culture that sustained it. Part III locates this as part of a larger political inquiry. And the Afterword contemplates what I have learned.

The book also follows an historical pattern. Part I covers the period from the earliest farming communities in the province to the establishment of Ontario cheddar as an export staple in the British imperial market. Part II covers the period from the turn of the century, when Ontario cheddar was at its height, through to the 1930s when the industry began to falter. Throughout this period, and beyond even into the 1950s, Ontario's cheese factories remained the centre of a vital rural culture. Part III covers the period from the end of the Second World War to the late 1970s, when Ontario cheddar was reduced to vestiges of living memory in the last of Ontario's cheesemaker-craftsmen. I interviewed many of these old men during the course of writing this book. Their voices, with their slow rural cadence, have much to teach us.

❦

Aberfeldy Farm
Glengarry County, Ontario

PART ONE
Origins and Continuities

Salford
Cheese Factory

Prologue

When I found the diary, it didn't matter that the name on the front was Walter Riddell — not some relative of mine. Housed in an institutional cardboard box at the Ontario Archives, it was musty with time and mildewed space. Wearing protective white cotton gloves, I removed the diary from the box. It was a small, hard-covered book, still in its dust jacket of mauve-striped shirt cloth stitched by hand with sturdy black thread. Inside, the pages were filled with rust-black ink, penned in a bold but meticulous script by 19-year-old Walter Riddell as he left his home in the Dumfries district of Southwestern Scotland in the spring of 1933. He set out on foot for Annan on the coast, where he boarded the wooden sailing ship the *Lancaster* for a two-month journey across the Atlantic Ocean to Quebec City and, from there, to Upper Canada. He kept voyage in his diary:

April 4: Left my father's house to go to America with feelings of deep regret, passed Old Hermitage Castle about 8 o'clock. . . .

April 20: Wind still ahead; some water breaking over our decks these two days.

April 21: A cold day; wind North; most of the passengers better . . . today the *Cherub* of Maryport crossed our tack, bound for Quebec with passengers. . . .

April 22: A fine day; lost sight of land about 8 a.m.; about 4 p.m. spoke to the *Forth* of Glasgow homeward bound — loaded with cotton. A swallow lighted on our deck.

April 23: A fine morning till about 12 when the day became cold and cloudy; about 4 p.m. a squall from the North West which broke our bowsprit boom.

April 24: A fine calm day. . . .

April 25: A wet morning til about about 8 a.m.; often saw a grampus (type of dolphin) today, the first of very many.

April 26: A wet morning; a heavy gale all day from the North West, the water breaking over the bows.

April 27: The weather still stormy from the North West — the water breaking over the decks.

April 28: Still stormy from the same quarter, and the water lashing over the decks. . . .

May 28: Saw 29 sail. It was really a fine sight to see so many of them all together and in full sail; passed about 12 of them before noon; about 7 p.m. spoke to the *Arno* of Workington from Sligo with passengers; she appeared to be very crowded. They had a very ragged appearance. . . .

June 1: Came to anchor about midnight on the Quarantine anchorage at Grosse Island. . . . *June 2:* About 5 p.m. the Inspector came on board of us and told us of the *Harvey* of Limerick with 35 passengers dead of cholera. She was lying close beside us. Our captain went ashore in the evening and brought us word of the loss of nine vessels amongst the ice. . . . *June 3:* Blew very hard from the East. . . . We ran foul of the *Harvey*, her bowsprit got entangled among our rigging, and, being a much larger vessel, almost came over us and battered us severely about the main cabins. . . . The time she was foul of us, the cries of the women and children were terrible and hurt us far worse than the ship, and I shall never forget it as long as I live. . . .

The truth of the matter was that settlement, and the needs of settlers, were secondary to the minds of the people running the colonies of British North America at the time. Their first priority was defending the border against the predatory Americans and their republican ideas. Their second priority was extracting whatever resources could be taken from the colonies and profitably sold in the commercial markets of England and Europe. The list had begun with fish and furs. By the early 1800s, it included timber from the still forest-bound colonies of British North America. Carrying emigrants to the Canadas was a convenience to the timber merchants whose ships were full only on the trip back to England.

Some emigrants could afford "cabin class" passage (at 18 pounds sterling, compared with seven pounds, 10 shillings for "steerage").[1] The cabin class included half-pay officers and their wives, such as John and Susanna Moodie, members of an emerging middle class who saw in emigration a chance to move up in the world. However, the vast majority travelled steerage, in makeshift quarters in the often unsanitary holds of the timber ships.[2]

Largely indifferent to them in transit (particularly by the 1820s and 1830s), the colonial administration remained that way once they'd cleared the Quarantine Station at Grosse Island, neglecting their needs for housing, education, transportation, communications, and even basic health care. In 1832, the peak year of emigration, 4,000 people died of the cholera in Montreal alone — one in nine of the population of around 36,000.[3]

Still the emigrants came on, wave after wave of them fleeing the wrenching dislocations of industrialization in the towns and cities, and the commercialization and mechanization of agriculture in the countryside. They came first seeking a chance just to survive, and then to improve their lot in the modern age of progress.

During the 1830s, a quarter of a million emigrants poured past Grosse Island and up the Gulf of St. Lawrence. Boarding paddlewheelers and steamboats at Quebec City, they travelled upriver to Montreal, commercial capital of the fur-trade, and beyond, through the rudimentary Soulange and Lachine canals to Lake Ontario. There they bought passage on paddlewheelers or flatbottom sailboats called Schenectadies, or on the smaller and cruder (but no doubt cheaper) Durham boats or row boats which took them as far as they could get by water. The Durhams were shod with iron for weathering the rapids and rocky shallow stretches. They were powered, like the batteaux, with poles which were passed from hand to hand down the length of the boat to draw it forward over rushing water.

This haphazard transport brought them to the old fur-trading forts of Frontenac (renamed Kingston) and Niagara, and to the Loyalist settlements at Cornwall, Lyndhurst (renamed Brockville), Belleville, Hamilton, and St. Catherines — all on Lake Ontario or the St. Lawrence River.

Inland from there, little had changed since the Ice Age when glaciers had left their mark on the face of what would be Ontario. Marauding ice sheets had scraped bare the Precambrian rock of the North and Northeast and scattered stones and gravel across the East and Central regions.[4] Then, as the glaciers retreated and the ice fields melted, they deposited the finest soil across the flatlands in the West and Southwest districts. The legacy was evident in the trees that blanketed the land. Cedar and swamp oak grew dwarfed and tangled on the thin, gravelly soils in the East. Sugar maple, butternut, elm, and beech grew thick in the heavy soils in the Central region. In the Southwest, pine, oak, hickory, basswood, and some black walnut announced that the sandy loam here was the richest and most workable land for farming.[5] A Sulpician priest travelling through the area in 1670 described it as "the terrestrial paradise of Canada."[6] Late Loyalists travelling westward by covered Connestoga wagon from Niagara followed what some of them called "the trail of the black walnut" into richly fertile Oxford County.[7]

The First Peoples of North America had farmed since about 3,500 B.C., beginning a simple corn-based horticulture in what is now Central America and Mexico. They developed some 300 corn varieties, which they traded northward into what is now Quebec and Ontario. When Jacques Cartier explored the St. Lawrence River in 1535, he recorded seeing large fields of corn under cultivation outside Indian villages.[8] In 1615, Samuel de Champlain found evidence of farming both among the Ottawas of Manitoulin Island and the Hurons around Lake Simcoe. There, he reported that the "largest part" of the land was "cleared up" and "thickly settled with a countless number of human beings," whose entire economy was centred on agriculture.[9]

Two hundred years later, much of that had vanished. Smallpox, measles, and other plagues contracted from Europeans during the fur-trade, combined with the "Indian wars" (involving rivalries in the fur trade and exploited by the traders for competitive advantage), had decimated the Native population and their agricultural base. Still, Native agriculture remained a vital presence. As historian Harold Innis has documented in his study of *The Fur Trade*, Indian corn was a staple in the diet of the fur-traders.[10] It also seems to have been a staple first crop among Ontario's settler farmers and might well have been critical for their survival after the colonial government stopped sponsoring settlers with rations and clearing tools in the 1820s.[11]

Emigrant settlers presented themselves at land offices, or boards, administered directly by colonial officials or indirectly through settlement and land company agents. There they were given a location ticket indicating what lot they could claim as their own. Often, the men made a preliminary trip into the bush to scout out this land, to clear an initial half acre, build a rough shanty, and plant a few seeds: corn, squash, and maybe some potatoes. This was a backwoods farm.

Settlers' shanty cabins were damp and drafty, with parchment animal-skin windows and bare-earth floors. Crude chimneys made of clay-mud and sticks leaked smoke into the room and often caught fire. Colds were common, and scurvy was prevalent; yet few knew the Indian custom of boiling the bark of white

Top: A Canadian emigrant's first home in the backwoods, circa 1862, reproduced from Catherine Parr Traill's *The Canadian Emigrant Housekeeper's Guide.* *Bottom:* Logging Bee in Perth County circa 1870.

cedar or the bark and needles of the black spruce for a restorative tonic.[12] Few also knew how to treat the ague with quinine or with the inner bark of the black cherry steeped in whisky.[13] The ague, or "swamp fever," is similar to malaria. It afflicted many of the pioneer settlements as trees were clear cut and flood waters rose, bringing plagues of ague-spreading mosquitoes. In one of the roughest scenes in her journal of backwoods survival, *Roughing It in the Bush*, Susanna Moodie describes being in labour with her fifth child while her husband and her youngest child were both incapacitated with the ague. Shortly after her baby was born, Susanna noted that her nurse's husband arrived and "carried his wife away upon his back, and I was left to struggle through in the best manner I could, with a sick husband, a sick child and a new-born babe."[14] She, too, suffered from the ague.

One account of early farms in Ontario notes that "women were old in their thirties, worn out by childbearing and exhausting drudgery. Malaria was nearly universal. Individuals died of 'decline,' of 'inflammation of the bowels,' of diphtheria and scarlet fever."[15]

There were few doctors in the backwoods. Even the few old-country healers and midwives often simply couldn't get to the sick because the roads were impassable. One account, from Glengarry County in Eastern Ontario, described local roads as "too thin to plow and too thick to drink."[16] In Perth County, roads of the early 1800s were "avoided by all travellers except those on foot."[17]

British travel writer Anna Brownell Jameson described her 1837 sojourn from Hamilton West towards Colonel Talbot's estate in outraged tones:

The roads were throughout so execrably bad that no words can give you an idea of them. We often sunk into mud-holes above the axle-tree. . . . About sunset I arrived at Blandford, dreadfully weary and fevered, and bruised, having been more than nine hours travelling twenty-five miles.

Worse was the isolation the poor roads produced, with single farms struggling to subsist surrounded by miles of unbroken forest, as Ann Jameson observed:

I remember particularly one of these clearings, which looked more desolate than the rest. No ground was fenced in, and the newly felled timber lay piled in heaps ready to burn; around lay the forest, its shadows darkening, deepening as the day declined. But what riveted my attention was the light figure of a female arrayed in a silk gown and a handsome shawl, who was pacing up and down in front of the house, with a slow step and pensive air. She had an infant lying on her arm, and in the other hand she waved a green bough to keep off the mosquitoes.[18]

Yet the isolation was largely man-made, resulting from two related causes. First, the government's feudal land-granting policies put too much land in the hands of titled military officers or wealthy merchants who comprised a self-styled local elite called the Family Compact. With the exception of Col. Talbot, who by 1831 had settled 30,000 emigrants on his grant of more than half a million acres, most of this gentry left the grants undeveloped. This, plus the lands set aside as clergy and Crown reserves to further support the local aristocracy, greatly retarded the land-settlement process because it created an artificial shortage of land for would-be settlers through the 1820s and 1830s and left the legitimate settlers struggling to survive in isolated clearings surrounded by uncleared land.

The second and related problem was the government's neglect of local transportation in favour of ships, canals, and such to facilitate the export of readily available resource staples to England. Transportation could have been geared to the needs of the settler communities scattered through the interior of the province, not just to the priorities of the export merchants. But it wasn't.

Both issues figured prominently in a survey of settlement problems in 1822. It was sponsored by an enlightened land agent called Robert Gourley, a graduate of the University of St. Andrews in Scotland who served on a government inquiry into pauperism prior to his emigration to Canada.[19] In his self-appointed township survey of Upper Canada, question number 31 asked people, "What in your opinion most retards the improvement of your township in particular and the province in general, and what would most contribute to same?" Over half of the citizens cited uncleared and unimproved lands of absentee landowners as the biggest obstacle to development. Forty-five per cent cited the nearly five million acres of clergy and Crown reserves. The reserves were generally left wild and therefore had no roadway cleared past them. Lack of capital and infrastructure were cited as the third and fourth grievances.[20]

The checkered pattern of settlement and roadwork aggravated the shortage of capital by restricting local economics to a subsistence level. It prevented people from marketing their produce and specializing in marketable products by which they could earn cash to pay the mortgage. As one observer put it, "the removal of standing trees to make a clear right of way was a necessary condition for commerce and also a sufficient one."[21] Through a combination of inadequate foreign capital and the tendency of local banks to finance trade and commerce, not agriculture, there was a chronic shortage of money for farming.[22] Farm mortgage rates ran as high as 12 to 15 per cent.[23] A British traveller hazarded a guess that "a forced collection of debts at this time would ruin two-thirds of the farmers in the province."[24]

Gourlay's research laid the foundation for the 1837 Rebellion by giving a public voice to the grievances of frustrated farmers, articulating them as a common systemic problem, not just the product of individual ill-fortune. It also broadened support for the changes being advocated by the Reformers. The Reformers wanted a democratic and egalitarian society, constitutionally grounded in the value of human labour, not capital and privileged title. As Reformer and Rebellion leader William Lyon MacKenzie put it to a meeting in the County of York: "Labour is the true source of wealth. . . . To produce this wealth, the farmer, the miller, the labourer, the sailor, the merchant, each contributes his share by useful industry in an honest calling."[25] In his draft constitution for the State of Upper Canada, he declared that labour should be the only means of creating wealth — not capital, from which the power and privileges of the commercial elites were derived.[26]

The Rebellion was over so fast and its supporters punished so severely that these ideas were driven underground for nearly a century.[27]

Business carried on as usual. Slowly, through local markets run by agricultural societies, as well as by local produce merchants, trade within the colony developed. Potash from clearing fires and maple sugar were often the settlers' first crops. They were traded, usually for goods, through produce merchants who exported the ash as fertilizer for the depleted soils of England. Lumber was also traded, sometimes for cash. As farms grew from an initial acre or two to five and 10 acres of cleared plowed land, wheat and other grains were grown in marketable quantities.[28] Gradually the commercial elite began to take notice of the farmers in the colony as an export market emerged for grain and, later, for cheddar cheese. A little money began to be spent in supporting the people living in the countryside, with grants for roads and schools, for agricultural societies and dairymen's associations.

Bush Farming, Bees, and Agricultural Societies

Walter Riddell's emigrant diary records that he was assigned Lot 27, 1st Concession, Hamilton Township, Northumberland County, to clear and settle. Then it stops. There's no record of what he did next: whether he cleared his land alone or with neighbours coming together in a local labour pool called a bee. Most accounts of bees depict them as drunken "brawls," a waste of time and money on the part of the sponsors.[1] Most

Residence of J.G. Giles, M.D., near Farmersville (now Athens), Ontario, circa 1879.

are also written by those with money enough to sponsor them. They might, therefore, include a certain class bias, much as accounts of settlement by upper-class figures such as John Galt, founder of the Canada Company, seem biased in an opposite direction.

In 1903, William Johnston began his *History of the County of Perth* as an epic:

History begins in this county in 1828 when John Galt and his band of explorers blazed a path through the trackless woods to that spot where Goderich now stands. This event was an insignia of a new dominion, and a new force pregnant with energy and an inherent power to conquer and subdue.[2]

The people who actually cleared the land were untitled and relatively unmonied people given grants of 100 or 200 acres, plus untold numbers of squatters, squatting "almost through self-defence."[3] For them, settlement was probably a lot less grand. Technological historian Norman Ball has argued that the ones who survived and prospered did so through patience, a long-term clearing plan, and a willingness to be modified by the land even as they modified it themselves. Many learned from the local Indians or the Yankees, who themselves had learned from the natives generations earlier. They didn't attempt to fell the largest trees, but girdled them, conserving their strength by chopping only the small and medium-sized trees. They also learned to choose, where possible, a well-designed Canadian or "common chopping" axe and to keep it well sharpened so it would continue to bite the wood, not bounce off against shins and feet.[4]

Working steadily, a reasonably fit man with a reasonably sharp axe could clear an acre in a fortnight.[5] That was often the extent of the first backwoods farm. Settlers then assembled the logs in a corner of the clearing, notching each to fit into the groove of the cross-laid one below. With the longer branches, they framed the door and possibly a hole for a window, plus the "rafters" for the lean-to roof. They thatched the smaller branches and the bark into a roof, somewhat in the manner of the Indians in the roofs of their longhouses. Finally, using a stick, or a mattock if they had one, they scratched some holes in the ground between the tree stumps and planted their first backwoods-farming crops: corn, and perhaps also beans, squash or pumpkins, plus perhaps some potatoes brought from home.[6]

Those who had money could hasten the settlement process by hiring choppers. County clearing records suggest that perhaps a quarter of the settlers did this.[7] The average immigrant of the time, however, was estimated to have only about 15 pounds sterling.[8] As a result, many probably did everything the slow way, by the tedium of their own labour either alone or in a round-robin of clearing bees through the neighbourhood.

With the initial clearing done, men whittled plowboards out of maple boughs and harrows out of sharpened sticks driven through branches arranged in a triangular frame.[9] Women made candles out of bulrushes stuck into bowls of animal fat. They made soap out of ashes. They ground corn in a mortar hollowed out of one of the charred stumps in the yard, using a pestle whittled out of black oak or other hardwood.[10] They made coffee from wild parsnip, and tea from wild wintergreen. They milked their one or two "bush cows," a local breed that could "stand starvation best" and survive on shoots sprouting from stumps and cut brush.[11] Some of this milk was mashed up with potatoes as a meal. Some was made into a primitive form of cheese, using a home preparation of rennet for curdling the milk, which had been placed by the open fireplace to warm.[12]

After 10 hard years of labour, a family might have 25 to 30 acres cleared. With wheat yields averaging about 20 bushels per acre and markets returning around 75 cents a bushel, they could begin to make some money. Enough to buy some cows and a pair of horses, to build a nice house, and even to hire some choppers to speed up clearing more land.[13]

By the 1840s, a number of asheries across the province were still turning the remnants of clearing fires into fertilizer for export, and these would continue in some parts of the province until the late 1800s. The timber trade still flourished, though it peaked in 1845.[14] Wheat had become a prime export staple by 1825 and, except for the bust years of the late 1830s, it would maintain its primary position through the Crimean War and even into the 1860s.[15] There were also hundreds of distilleries and drinking establishments, which attests to the widespread drinking, by the men at least, as a release from the "hard and monotonous" life in the bush.[16]

Even while wheat, timber and other primary-product exports flourished, many farmers were diversifying into cattle and into the crafts of butter and cheese making. Year after year through the 1840s and 1850s, the growth of these crafts could be measured at the local agricultural fairs and exhibits, where steadily more classes and ranks of produce were brought for exhibit and sale.

The agricultural fairs and societies extended the tradition of pooling labour and rural self-reliance. Agricultural fairs were also a way of developing a domestic economy while trading farm produce and household manufactures. A proclamation advertising the first Agricultural Fair in Glengarry County in 1802 states that its purpose was: "for superfluities which might be turned to greater advantage by being sold or bartered within [the county] than being disposed of, even at a higher price, in the lower province, considering the loss of time consequent on going thither and the perpetual drain of money which the country suffers by depending solely upon the Montreal market."[17]

The county agricultural societies, which organized these fairs and exhibits, were perhaps the most important institutions for sharing knowledge and promoting agricultural "improvements" in the early days of Ontario.[18] An offspring of the agricultural revolution that propelled farming from subsistence to a commercial scale in Britain in the 16th century, agricultural societies served as rural schools and even as learned and literary societies; some societies offered a prize for the best paper or essay presented, and published them as well.

In their heyday, membership included physicians, politicians, merchants, and clergymen — as well as freehold or yeomen farmers, all of whom saw themselves as part of the emerging middle class. Although Lord Simcoe helped launch the first society in 1792 by donating some prize money and a set of books for its library, government support for these institutions didn't really begin until the 1830s.[19] Then the government guaranteed an annual grant of 100 pounds to societies once they had raised at least 50 pounds through local subscriptions.[20]

The by-laws establishing the first agricultural society in Northumberland County read in part: "resolved to found a joint-stock farmers' bank of intelligence and experience upon which the agricultural population of the country might draw *ad libitium*."[21]

Walter Riddell attended that founding meeting. It was held sometime in 1836 at a typical meeting place of the day, Arkland's Tavern. He put down the five shillings the farmers had agreed to establish as the annual dues and volunteered to serve as treasurer. He held that post for 35 years, while the membership grew to 73 members by 1860 and 215 by 1871. He did this, he wrote later, "for neither fee nor fame nor praise . . . but I thought it a duty to do what I could to improve and further the farming interests of the neighbourhood." It was a sentiment not everyone shared, it seemed, as he noted in a paper on the history of the Northumberland Agricultural Society: "A little more public spirit and a little less local jealousy and a little more liberality would greatly conduce to the better working of all our agricultural institutions."

Riddell gave many papers at society meetings over the years, sprinkling his texts with references from the Bible and Greek and Roman classics. In a paper on root crops, he noted that Pliny was reputed to have grown turnips. He began that paper with the homily, "More roots, more stock; more stock, more manure; more manure better crops."

Another paper begins:

There is no subject that is so pressing on the farmers at the present time, that requires so much of his care and thought as the destruction of weeds. So pressing is this matter that it seems if we cannot subdue the weeds, they will conquer us, and prevent us reaping any crops at all. The land cannot grow a large crop of grain and a large crop of weeds at the same time. As the earth is the mother of the weeds but only the step-mother of our crops, it is the crops that suffer.[22]

By 1855, there were 40 agricultural societies and at least 150 township ones. The men and women who'd been swallowed up by the wilderness in the early years of the century were producing corn, wheat, cider, wool, and even cheese enough to register volumes in the first agricultural census of Upper Canada. They thronged to the society affairs, exhibiting and competing where they had a specialty, admiring, learning, and buying where they lacked. At one, a newspaper correspondent wrote glowingly of a plowing match, a feature of many fall fairs, which served to demonstrate the latest hand-forged plows as well as local skill and technique in plowing: "Our mind was carried back to the palmy days of Greece when . . . her best and bravest sons joined in the public games and contended with all their might. How much more praiseworthy is it in those who come out . . . to further the improvement of agriculture."[23]

The biggest prizes were in livestock breeding, especially for stallions and bulls. Prizes were also given for the best wheat, oats, barley, peas, potatoes, and Indian corn. There were prizes for identifying the best ways of adapting different manures for different kinds of soil and prizes for giving the best paper on aspects of plant and animal husbandry. In the huge category of "home" or "domestic" manufactures (this in the days before factories), there were prizes for farm implements.[24] In 1851, Daniel Massey exhibited a mowing machine he'd forged at his Newcastle Foundry and Machine Co. in Northumberland County. Three years later, this second-generation Loyalist exhibited a reaper that replaced four men toiling through the August fields with hand-held scythes and turkey cradles. It would revolutionize farming in Upper Canada by helping to boost its scale to commercial proportions. In 1891, Massey and his son formed a partnership with the Harris family of implement manufacturers to found Massey-Harris, which later became a multinational corporation trading well on the stock market.[25]

In other home manufactures, there were prizes for the best hand-made cheese presses and butter moulds, for dower boxes and kitchen utensils, for linen, flannel, homespun and wool, for soap and candles and maple sugar, and for home-made beer, butter, and cheese.

In Oxford County, first prize for cheese consistently went to Hiram Ranney, although everyone knew it was his wife, Lydia Chase Ranney, who actually made the cheese.

Women Cheesemakers and Their Craft

Recorded history moves in quantum leaps and paradigm shifts. Changes are neat as chapter headings, tailored to prevailing theories and theorists, with ill-fitting threads summarily snipped away.

Most accounts of Ontario dairying begin in 1864 and credit Harvey Farrington from Herkimer County, New York, as Ontario's "pioneer" cheesemaker. Before then, it was assumed, cheesemaking was pursued largely on a subsistence level using only "primitive technology."[1] It wasn't a specialized craft, but simply one of women's many chores. When the Ontario Agriculture Department, and the dairy industry, celebrated Ontario's cheese centennial, the year was 1964 and the focus was on cheesemaking in public commercial factories, not in family-farm dairies and local agricultural fairs. The "official" history of cheesemaking in Ontario begins with an account of how men and public corporations took over the craft and transformed it into an "industry" which conformed to prevailing theories about industry, including a commercial orientation and patented, not home-made, technology.

Only a few stray threads would seem to challenge that account. A few names pop up in unconventional sources: in a summer employment project celebrating the Women of Oxford County, done by a women's group;[2] more in a hand-written account of cheesemaking penned by James Crawford, a cheesemaker in the 1860s;[3] something else in an article published by the Women's Institute.[4] There's also the evidence of the 1861 agricultural census. Through township after township, in Oxford County at least, the census papers show small volumes of butter produced on virtually every farm; this is consistent with the "subsistence" pattern. But in the cheese column, the majority of farms show no cheese production whatsoever. Then there's a farm, and often a small cluster of farms, where production exceeded three tons. These stray threads form the fabric of a fascinating story.

Elizabeth (Eliza) Elliott and her family emigrated from England in 1833 and settled in the district of West Zorra, Oxford County. In 1845, she married a fellow English emigrant, Charles Wilson, and moved to a farm Charles had signed to purchase from a local landowner, William Barker, for $100 down and $100 a year for the duration of the mortgage. The first shock was discovering that their 100 partially cleared acres had been sold and repossessed three times previously and that the buildings that Barker had said were on it in fact lay outside the property line. The second occurred when Eliza's father, who'd given two heifers for his daughter's dowry, came by one day. Seeing one of them looking big and ready to calve, he decided to take this one back.

But Eliza needed her cow. With the two heifers from Charles' father and her own, plus three more the newlyweds had bought themselves, they were hoping to start a dairy which would help them pay off the mortgage. Eliza planned to make cheese, which Charles could market in London. So when her father commenced driving the heifer down the lane, she ran ahead and herded the beast back home. Whereupon she locked the gate against her father and kept her herd intact.

An account of her life as a pioneer cheesemaker in Oxford County continues the story:

Apparently, Mrs. Wilson made excellent cheese, for soon one buyer contracted for all she could produce. When the time came to make the payment on the mortgage, they took the $100 plus interest to Mr. Barker's home, but he refused to take the money. He had fully expected to take the farm back and resell it. The Wilsons placed the money on his table and left. So against his will, Barker was forced to accept. They continued to meet their payments and eventually owned the farm.

By the 1850s, Eliza Wilson was making cheese for her neighbours as well as herself. To achieve this scale, she had the local cooper (simply, a maker of containers such as casks, tubs, and pails) make her a set of buckets, tubs, and a vat. The vessels must have been quite large, for it is said that "when she became exasperated with a rather indolent helper she seized him by the collar and tossed him into the whey vat."[5]

The 1861 agricultural census reveals that in Oxford County, 43 farms produced over a ton of cheese a year. Many farms produced many times that. The Charles Wilson farm was listed with 8,000 pounds of cheese, while Leonard Wilson on the farm next door was listed with 6,000, and a Robert Wilson down the road had 2,000. There are many farms with cheese production of around 15,000 pounds, such as John Adams of the district of East Nissouri and Henry Smith and Andes Smith of North Norwich. But Hiram and Lydia Chase Ranney of Dereham Township were in a class by themselves, producing 30,000 pounds of cheese, while their son Homer, now on a farm of his own, produced 16,000.

Lydia and Hiram Ranney had developed a prosperous little dairy in Vermont, from which they sold butter and cheese into the Boston market. However, in 1830 they agreed to guarantee a neighbour's debts, and the neighbour (Lydia's brother in some accounts) defaulted. The creditors seized the Ranneys' farm and everything on it. With only a few personal items and their children — Hiram-Henry, Homer, and Julia — Lydia and Hiram Ranney travelled north to find free land in Canada, settling first in the

Lydia Ranney at the age of 92.

The Ranney homestead, Salford, Ontario, where Lydia made cheese and operated her dairy school.

Eastern Townships. Three years later, they moved on. They travelled three weeks along the coach road from Montreal to York, then weeks more on the often intractable paths south and west from there. At a lodging house at Hagel's Corners in Norwich Township, Oxford County, the proprietor, Peter Hagel, urged the family to stay. Schooling in the district was still in the crudest stages, with children (and adults too) gathering at the home of whomever had some books and could read a little and write. If Mrs. Ranney would agree to teach school, Hagel is reported to have said, the Hagels would help the family get settled on a farm. It was agreed. Mrs. Ranney rode on horseback to Hamilton to obtain the necessary certificate and became the first official school teacher in the township.[6]

Normally, families paid two dollars per quarter for each child taught and boarded the teacher around. But the Ranneys took Lydia's pay in the form of help, clearing land, raising buildings and, a little later, doing the barnyard chores. "With everything they could barter, they acquired cattle," local historian Art Williams recorded later. Within the first year, Lydia was milking three cows and working the milk up into cheese and butter for Hiram to peddle in London. Within four years, the herd had grown to 25, as many as they'd had in Vermont.

Lydia quit teaching and, with Julia's help, devoted herself to cheesemaking. Soon, neighbours were asking if their daughters could learn cheesemaking from her as well, and she started a dairy school. There were as many as 14 dairy maids at a time both learning from her and helping in the increasingly large home dairy. One of her secrets was scrupulously high standards. As Art Williams wrote, "Lydia Ranney was a particular woman, and the girls who studied and worked under her found that she had one grade, and that was perfect."[7]

Another secret lay in the improvements she, and other women like her, were making to both the technique of making cheese and its technology. Farm cheese making hadn't changed very much from the days of backwoods farming in the early 1800s. Small lots of milk were set in a washtub or other large, open container either in front of the open fireplace or atop the cook-stove. When heated to a point that suggested a certain degree of fermenting had occurred, the milk was then "set" by adding rennet or wild artichoke. The curdled milk was then cut up and allowed to "cook" in the solution of hot whey, at the same time being stirred with a wooden paddle or rake. The curds were then strained off in a "curd basket" made of braided bark in which loose-woven cloth ("cheesecloth") was draped. This in turn was set into a wooden frame called a cheese "ladder," which was placed over a bucket to catch the dripping whey. Once the curds were drained, salt was added to stop the fermenting and help preserve the cheese. Then the curds were dumped into a home-made "press" consisting of a cylindrical wooden container called a cheese "hoop" and a wooden lid that went down inside it called a folla or follower. These in turn were set in a wooden frame with a lever fixed to the top. The lever's action pushed the folla down hard against the curds, pressing out the remaining whey onto a wooden drainboard.[8] Pressing out the whey was essential for making a good firm cheese, not the loose and gassy "stink cheese" of backwoods farm repute.

Lydia Chase Ranney modified local cheese-making techniques in a number of ways, including the technique, developed in England, of "cheddaring" the cheese curd. Having allowed the curds to mat after the initial draining off of the whey, she cut them up, then scalded them with reheated whey. This drew out more of the whey. She then put the curds back onto the draining rack, cooled them with cold water, and left them to drain for another hour. Finally, she ran them through her home-made curd mill, salted them, and packed them into cheese hoops for pressing.[9]

Both Lydia Chase Ranney and Eliza Wilson found ways to improve the mechanical force of the cheese press to squeeze out the last of the whey and pack the cheese curds firmly together. Mrs. Wilson hung a bucket full of rocks at one end of a pole, the other end of which was wedged against the lever; this greatly increased both the pressure that could be exerted against the folla and, equally important, the time it could be maintained.

The Ranneys' technology, it seems, went a step further. Rather than using a lever, which transfers force from one place to another and augments it only slightly, they used a winch or a windlass, which multiplies force considerably. Whether it had been used for cheese pressing before the Ranney's innovation isn't known. Certainly, the windlass was widely used in that era — on sailing ships, for hauling up well water, and in the rocky farmlands of Eastern Ontario for pulling up tree stumps and stones. A sketch of the Ranney's device, which Hiram would likely have built himself, shows a series of ropes (possibly with pulleys too) running from the top to the bottom of the cheese press, knotted at the top into an axle with a pole-handle sticking out of it for turning. As the axle was turned, winding up the rope, the top and bottom of the press would be pulled tighter together, causing the folla to press ever harder against the cheese curds inside it.

It could well have been the combination of this technology and Lydia's meticulous cheese-making which made the Ranneys' cheese so successful. By the 1850s, with a herd of 100 cows supplying the farm factory, Hiram had a regular route selling cheese to import-export merchants in Hamilton, London, and Guelph, taking four days to complete his rounds. The Ranneys also made the first local "mammoth"

A cheese press with ropes and windlass to press the whey from the curds held in the wooden hoop or folla.

cheeses. Ranging from 1,000 to 1,200 pounds, they won first prize at the Oxford Agricultural Society fair in 1848 and for many years thereafter.[10] One 1,200-pound mammoth was apparently sent to England, where it "sold at a remunerative price."[11]

James Crawford was 80 years old in 1926 when he sat down to write his memoires of working as a cheesemaker in Oxford County during the 1860s:

Of all those who began the cheese business in Canada, I think it would not be out of place to mention one of these good farmers' wives because of the fame which her cheese received. This lady was Mrs. Hiram Ranney who began making cheese at a very early date in the 19th century with the milk of three cows. . . . Mrs. Ranney and her assistant Robert Facey were the people who laid the cornerstone of the dairy industry in Canada by their successful prosecution of that great and important branch of husbandry which has proved to be for the general prosperity of the country.[12]

Women remained a vital presence in cheese-making until the end of the century. Some worked as cheesemakers in their own farm dairies, as these continued to contribute a significant proportion of the province's cheese output. Others were employed in the new public factories as "assistants." The simultaneous exclusion and persistence of women in cheese-making shows up in comical ways. A history of the Dairymen's Association of Western Ontario reported that "the new cheesemaking industry was facing many other obstacles" besides poor-quality cheese. "One big objection was from the womenfolk who up to the time of commercial factories had control over the milk, yet these same factories were giving them a new freedom away from drudgery." Later, in a section on local cheese fairs and their role in improving cheese quality during the 1870s, the author reported that "a notable feature of this advance in quality was the big part taken by some ladies. It has been recorded that one young lady, Miss Mary Morrison, won the most coveted awards as top cheesemaker."[13]

Another account, testifying to the enduring presence of women cheesemakers, reports that there were two Morrison sisters, each of whom took top prizes for their cheese at various exhibitions. Both operated cheese factories, one at Newry and the other at Harriston, and did so "until well into the 20th century."[14]

A history of the Sterling Creamery, also pays brief homage to a woman cheesemaker. "Madoc pioneer Annie Elevier, great-grand-mother of the present owners, won the award for the highest scoring cheese at the Chicago World Fair in 1893. She taught the art to her husband and their sons. One of the sons, William C. West, had been the cheesemaker at Harold and Stockdale before he got into the butter business."[15]

The invisibility of women in the history of dairying has been noted by others and at least partially corrected.[16] But few people understand the significance of women's contributions. Factory cheesemaking in Canada was a continuation of farm cheesemaking and rested solidly on women's home-made technology — not imported American technology as the official history suggests.

In his Introduction to *The Dairy Industry in Canada*, economic historian Harold Innis (who grew up on a farm in Oxford County) states that "the cheese-making . . . techniques and institutions" were all imported from the United States. As one often-quoted example, Innis notes that, in 1870, Robert Facey brought the hot-iron test for detecting when the acid in the cheese curd had developed enough from New York State into Canada.[17] Innis' writings credit none of the technology developed by women in local farm dairies. It isn't that these technologies didn't exist. Rather, they weren't recognized any more than women's cheesemaking was recognized as an "industry." Neither what they were doing nor the techniques and tools they were using fit the prevailing theories about "manufacturing industry" — namely a public and commercial enterprise employing patented commercial technology and, incidentally, run by men. So the commercial Oneida vats, imported from the U.S., feature heavily in accounts of early cheesemaking; yet the Ranneys' technology was equal to that of the Americans, according to an account in *Canada Farmer* (7 February 1864). Their technology must have included vat-like containers for making cheese, given the factory-like scale of their production.

Cheesemaking entrepreneur David Murdoch MacPherson, who learned cheesemaking from his step-mother Phoebe Marjerrison,[18] is credited with developing a lot of cheesemaking technology. However, it's likely that this involved transforming a lot of home-made technologies improvised and improved over the years by women like Mrs. Ranney, Mrs. Wilson, and his step-mother into patented manufactured products. He patented a curd rake, used for stirring curd in the curd-curing phase of cheesemaking, which it sold widely across Canada and the U.S. and even in New Zealand.[19] He patented a curd mill, rather similar to the description of one used by Lydia Chase Ranney.[20] He also patented a cheese box and formed a partnership with a local manufacturer to mass produce them.

A lot goes missing between oral and written versions of history, especially as the latter survives the former. A lot is also lost, or misplaced, between the official renderings of history and the unofficial accounts laid down in diaries and letters and occasionally in folklore.

The Cheese Poet of Oxford County

James McIntyre, the "Cheese Poet of Oxford County," is ridiculed in Canadian literature courses as one of Canada's worst poets. William Arthur Deacon, who launched the cult of disparagement with his anthology of 19th-century poets called *The Four Jameses*, singled out the worst examples of McIntyre's verse and quoted lines out of context only to mock them. McIntyre himself would have been surprised at having achieved such notoriety and, probably, dismayed at having been so badly misinterpreted.

McIntyre was 14 when he emigrated from Scotland, on his own, in 1841.[1] From his first job as farm labourer, he worked up to owning a funeral parlour with a coffin- and furniture-making business in Stratford. This in turn supported his family and his real vocation, poetry. It was modest, journeyman's work, published in the local paper and in a collection which he brought out himself. He wasn't trying to write Great Poetry. He wanted to honour the achievements of people like himself, who had come to this country with little or nothing, hoping to make new lives for themselves in British North America. Parochial poetry, published in the local paper, was one of the most accessible local media for doing this.

This "folk poetry," as it's called, helped interpret the rural community to itself and bind it together in a shared world view and ethos. As such, McIntyre and others like him made important contributions to Canadian folk culture through their verses.[2] For folklore historian Pauline Greenhill, folk poetry is not meant to be separated from the context of a particular local community. Also, it must be understood as process as well as product: a sort of ongoing dialogue between the poet and the community, in which the poet brings order out of the minutiae of everyday life through verses. By the title and content of the poems, the folk poet implicitly names what is "appropriate" and symbolically important to readers.

Not surprisingly, the progress myth emerges as perhaps the strongest theme in McIntyre's poems. A particular blending of the protestant ethic and the cult of modern science and technique, this mythology fired the imaginations of emigrant settlers. And it provided a mental model by which they could understand the drudgery of land-clearing and backwoods farming as the heroic project of "nation building."[3]

McIntyre's epic poem, "A Canadian Romance," is considered to be largely autobiographical:

James McIntyre, The Cheese Poet of Oxford County.

He knew a labourer he would be
Forever in the old country,
His forefathers had tilled the ground
And never one had saved a pound.

Their one luxury around their door,
A few choice flowers their garden bore
But never hoped to own the soil
But serve as hinds to sweat and toil.
To work and toil for him had charm
He hoped some day to own a farm.[4]

"Life in the Backwoods" is also typical of his work:

Canada hath wealthy yeomen
Whose fathers overcame the foeman;
The enemy they boldly slew
Was mighty forest they did hew,
And where they burned heaps of slain
Their sons now reap the golden grain.[5]

He wrote several poems in praise of local cheesemaking and the economic strength it gave to the farming community as demand for dairy products rose faster than the local supply and farmers made some money.

The "Oxford Cheese Maker's Song" is an ode to Hiram Ranney of Salford:

When Father Ranney left the States
In Canada to try the fates

He settled down in Dereham
Then no dairyman lived near him.
He was the first there to squeeze
His cows' milk into good cheese,
And at each Provincial Show
His famed cheese was all the go.

(Chorus)
Then long life to Father Ranney
May he wealth and honour gain, aye!

He always took the first prize,
Both for quality and size;
But many of his neighbours
Now profit from his labors.
And the ladies dress in silk
From the proceeds of the milk:
But those who buy their butter,
"How dear it is" they mutter.[6]

Part local historian, part myth-maker, McIntyre documented the forces shifting local agriculture from a wheat to a cheese economy. He did this best perhaps in "The Oxford Cheese Ode":

The ancient poets ne'er did dream
That Canada was land of cream,
They ne'er imagined it could flow
In this cold land of ice and snow,
Where everything did solid freeze,
They ne'er hoped or looked for cheese.
A few years since our Oxford farms

Were nearly robbed of all their charms,
O'er cropped the weary land grew poor
And nearly barren as a moor,
But now their owners live at ease
Rejoicing in their crop of cheese.

And since they justly treat their soil,
Are well rewarded for their toil,
The land enriched by goodly cows
Yields plenty now to fill their mows
Both wheat and barley, oats and peas,
But still their greatest boast is cheese.[7]

Wheat remained the dominant source of farmers' income until Confederation. However, constant wheat cropping was wearing out the soil the way it had in the lower province some time earlier. By 1851, yields had dropped to 16 bushels an acre, compared with 25 to 35 bushels in 1821.[8] Equally devastating was the wheat midge, which began to plague farms through the late 1840s. Poor crops in the late 1850s, coupled with the depression following the Crimean war, pushed more farmers into raising cattle. Many stayed at that stage of development, exporting live cattle into the lucrative American market of the 1860s. This ended abruptly in 1866, when the Americans moved toward protectionism after the Civil War by cancelling the Reciprocity Treaty. By this time, though, many farmers had established dairies, and more were making cheese. Production of cheese and butter increased by 60 per cent between 1851 and 1861, to 42 tons.[9] In Oxford County alone, cheese production exceeded two-and-a-half million pounds a year by 1861, with at least some portion of this being regularly exported to Britain.[10]

James McIntyre, the cheese poet would rise to even loftier heights of poetic exuberance when the sons and unnamed daughters of Oxford County's pioneers produced the world's largest mammoth cheese as a promotional stunt to help launch one of Ontario's most successful and enduring institutions. He saw in the cheese mammoth the ultimate symbol of progress, combining local hand labour and scientific technology in the modern pursuit of "industry."

Harvey Farrington and Industrialization

By 1860, farmers no longer cultivated five or 10 acres, but 50, 100, and more — and sent their wares to market. Local towns and villages were more than the grist mill, the forwarding merchant, and the ubiquitous wayside tavern. There was a school and a church and, sometimes, a town hall too. A range of industries thrived on serving the farm community:

blacksmiths and coopers, tanners and butchers, a lumber mill and furniture factory, and so on.[1] Each new enterprise, each side of beef, each bushel of grain, or pound of butter or cheese was an entry in the ledger book of progress.

But most entries paled next to the railway for combining personal progress and nation building, and the metaphors ran both ways. A railway promoter, Thomas Keefer wrote a pamphlet extolling the "civilizing tendency of the locomotive."[2] Newspapers of the day bemoaned the deadlocked government of the day with phrases like "wheels stuck fast" and, in 1867, allowed that "the machinery of government is all new, and it will take some time to get it properly in motion."[3]

During the railway boom of the 1850s and 1860s, track-lines in Canada West advanced from 55 miles to 3,000 miles by 1867. In 1854, the Great Western Railway was completed between Niagara Falls, Hamilton, London, and Windsor. In 1856, the Grand Trunk Railway opened its main line between Montreal and Toronto, then extended it west through Perth and Oxford Counties to Sarnia.[4] Suddenly, farmers in the hinterlands of Canada West had an entree into lucrative metropolitan markets, both in Canada and abroad. Suddenly, too, the commercial interests, which had invested heavily in railway expansion, had a vested interest in marketing whatever agricultural produce they could carry in their freight cars and thence onto their fleet of sailing ships. When the English boycotted American cheese imports as a means of snubbing the Yankees in the American Civil War, Canadian interests seized the opportunity.

One day in the spring of 1863, the train brought a Yankee newcomer to Ingersoll — Harvey Farrington. A teacher, a farmer, and also a cheesemaker, Farrington had helped establish cheesemaking on a factory scale back home in Herkimer County in New York State in the early 1850s.[5] This not only involved some different technology — principally a specially designed vat for making the milk up into cheese — it was also organized differently, as a "cooperative," where a number of farmers manufactured the cheese collectively, with a cheesemaker hired to do the specialized work. There were 38 factories across Herkimer County by 1856. Farrington, in partnership with a Mr. Harry Burrell, was said to have opened the third one.[6]

In 1863, he travelled by train north from New York to Ingersoll to visit some friends in the vicinity. It isn't known whether his motive was to save himself and his 10 children from the Civil War, which had begun two years earlier. It could have been for more practical reasons: seeking another means of exporting cheese to England. As well, the war had increased demand for cheese in the United States, and the Canadas were in the best position to fill it.

Whatever the reasons, the twice-widowed, homely little Mr. Farrington, who once described cheesemaking as his "calling," decided to immigrate to Canada and start a local cheese factory. He rented 10 acres on the farm of G.V. DeLong at Norwich and let a contract to Hiram Van Valkenburg to build him a two-storey factory roughly 50 feet long and 30 feet wide. It had a curing house of about the same size beside it, with living quarters for his family upstairs. He installed two vats and other equipment either imported from New York State or patterned after it by enterprising local manufacturers.[7] By the spring of 1864, he began making cheese for the farmers who had promised the milk of their cows as a pool of supply.

On November 1, the *Canada Farmer* carried a reprint from the *Hamilton Spectator* describing Mr. Farrington's factory: "a plain, neat-looking wooden building, not costing we should imagine over $100 complete. Double vats on the ground floor processing over 500 gallons of milk, delivered twice daily." The whey was fed to the pigs kept in a pen outside. The article counted 200 cheeses in the curing room, all slated for export. Each would return 20 cents a pound, minus two cents charged by Farrington for salt, cheesecloth bandages, and other supplies. Calculating further, the article reckoned the return for each farmer, with the milk of 10 cows each in the pool, at about $12.50 cash money a week — enough to meet the mortgage payment. "As to

Harvey Farrington, founding father of the cheddar cheese industry.

Commemorative cairn erected at Norwich, Ontario.

1864

ON A SITE ACROSS THE STREET FROM THIS CAIRN STOOD THE FIRST COMMERCIAL CHEESE FACTORY IN CANADA. IT WAS BUILT AND OPERATED 100 YEARS AGO BY HARVEY FARRINGTON.

1964

James Harris Cheese Factory, Ingersoll, Ontario, circa 1872, now the site of the Elm Hurst Inn.

the cheese," the report concluded with a nice colonial flourish, "we can vouch for its being quite equal to any American cheese we have tasted."[8]

Another edition of the *Canada Farmer* carried a report on dairying in Oxford County, based on visits to the farms of Hiram Ranney and James Harris. In Dereham Township, the editor wrote, "a most neighbourly feeling seems to exist among the dairy farmers, none feeling that the others are rivals, and all regarding Mr. Hiram Ranney with special respect as the dairy patriarch of the region."[9] The editor noted that Mr. and Mrs. Ranney had made a tour of cheese factories in upper New York state a year or two previously and had returned home satisfied that, except for a new technique for turning cheeses in the curing room, their operation needed no improvement. At the time, they were making between 14 and 18 tons of cheese a year. And up the road near Ingersoll, their son-in-law James Harris was making nine or ten tons a year. As was the "custom" of the day, the credit went to James, son of one of the Harris families brought to settle the area by Thomas Ingersoll under Lord Simcoe's feudal township settlement scheme. However, the cheesemaker was very likely his wife Julia, Lydia Ranney's daughter. When Harris started to expand in the late 1860s, taking in other farmers' milk and opening up branches,[10] he hired a cheesemaker from Herkimer County, a man by the name of H. Eldred.[11]

Farm-made cheese had become an "industry" in its own right before the advent of the cheese factory for some simple economic reasons. While merchants took in butter for barter, they paid hard cash for cheese. With the growth of this industry, a subtle shift occurred from the making of cheese itself towards making money from cheesemaking. A certain dependency was also introduced: dependency on patented, commercial technologies, the manufacturers of which brought to the new cheese industry a vested interest in making bigger and more capital-intensive technology. Slowly but inexorably, the commercial bias introducing this new phase of industrialization boosted the scale of operation. In the early years, however, this expansion was limited to the rather clumsy form of combine operations, where one person would own or control a string of small cheese factories. The twin handicap of still nearly impassable rural roads and lack of refrigeration kept individual factories small, with farmers living no farther than two or three miles (later, five) from the nearest cheese factory.

With reports of farmers "making money hand over fist" from participating in cheese-making milk pools, factory cheesemaking became a craze.[12] Within a year, there were three new factories in Oxford County, and Farrington had tripled his production to 30 tons.[13] The following year, Farrington built a second factory and, a year later, a third.[14] By 1867, there were some 235 factories across the province,[15] including one called "The Front of Sidney," near Belleville, another in Leeds County at Farmersville (later renamed Athens), and at least one in Perth County built by Thomas Ballantyne, a school teacher and farmer originally from Peebles, Scotland.[16]

A letter to the editor in the *Canada Farmer*, June 15, 1865, hints at the boosterism that accompanied the boom — although sales to the U.S. and England were a real enough reason for excitement. The letter describes "the very latest improvements" to James Harris's new factory just south of Ingersoll, noting that the new equipment "is good evidence that Canada is marching on in the race of improvement." Cheese buyers, the letter continues, are "as plentiful as flies in August, and already several offers have been refused from European shippers."[17]

Alluding to the devastations of the wheat midge and the general depression of the wheat market that had occurred since the late 1850s, the correspondent concludes by urging readers to "send your milk to a factory where you can have it manufactured for two cents a pound, thereby saving all expenses and paraphernalia of manufacturing. The milk crop never fails. For a more full knowledge of this factory, please to call at Ingersoll, and either Mr. Harris or his cheesemaker Mr. Eldred, will take pains to show you through the establishment."

By 1870, there were 322 factories across the

province, most of them located in Oxford, Elgin, and Middlesex counties.[18] Through the 1870s, expansion shifted eastward, into the poorer ground of Eastern Ontario, which nevertheless made durable pastureland. During the 1870s, 133 factories were started in Leeds and Hastings counties. The Plum Hollow Factory was built in the late 1870s and survived into the 1980s. At Forfar, the first factory was built on John Gile's farm in 1865; it became the Forfar Dairy in the 1960s, the last of the original craft-scale cheddar cheese factories operating in the region today.

Eighty-nine more were added in the 1880s, when expansion moved farther eastward.[19] The Balderson Cheese factory, which endured for over a century, was built at Balderson's Corners in 1881, on a lot purchased from Natt Balderson, one of founding settler families in Lanark County.[20] During that decade, 103 factories were built in Glengarry County alone.[21] Touring this district towards the end of the 1880s, the deputy minister of agriculture reported that "a new feeling was in the community. The farmers had progressed and they were comparatively well to do; everything was on the uplift and the whole thing was due to the fact that dairying had been brought in there, and had progressed along proper lines."[22]

By the turn of the century, there were over 1,000 cheese factories across Ontario and 2,500 cheesemakers. It was a rural commonplace that "the cheese factory paid the mortgage."

The organization of factories took a number of forms, depending on the spread or concentration of local wealth and the values of the people involved. In the western part of the province, which remained the centre of cheese-making until the early 20th century, there was a mix of private factories and cooperatives. James Harris established seven branch factories which made cheese from about 2,000 cows, and delivered it to his main facility outside Ingersoll for curing and storage.[23] Harvey Farrington also owned several factories; however, he actively promoted the cooperative or pooled system of operation whereby farmers retain ownership of the milk-cheese and the cheesemaker charged a set fee per pound for making it into cheese for them. Thomas Ballantyne of neighbouring Perth County, who became a prominent figure in the Dairymen's Association and a member of the provincial cabinet, also promoted cooperative milk pools. Ballantyne had managed a co-op store in Peebles, Scotland, before emigrating in 1852, becoming first a school teacher and then a farmer. He opened the Black Creek Cheese Factory in 1867, running it on Farrington's cooperative lines; his cheese exporting business, however, was strictly a private corporation.

In Eastern Ontario, development took a unique form, at least partly because of economic disparities. While some families had a lot of money — derived profits from the lumber trade in the Ottawa Valley or, earlier, from the fur trade with the NorthWest Company[24] — most farmers had little or nothing. Much of the expansion was a variation of the branch or chain ownership pioneered by James Harris and Harvey Farrington in Oxford County. One person, or a company of people called a syndicate or combine, owned a large number of factories. Most consisted of from 10 to 30 factories. The owners included D.G. McBean of Lancaster, W.D. McLeod of Kirkhill, William Eager and Thomas McDonald of Morrisburg, and J.H. Singleton of Smith Falls.[25] However, D.M. MacPherson of Lancaster came to be known as the champion of them all, earning the nickname "The Cheese King of Glengarry County" by building his Allengrove combine up to 80 factories spread across Glengarry County in Ontario and Huntington County in Quebec, where cheesemaking was rapidly becoming a major industry at this time as well. MacPherson, who made cheese on his family farm, the Allengrove, and whose diaries attest to his direct involvement in the craft, married Margaret McBean from a Montreal family with business connections in Lancaster in 1871.[26] To supervise the cheesemaking in all these factories, he hired James Ruddick, an Oxford County cheesemaker who later became federal Dairy Commissioner — and an outspoken critic of combines. Then MacPherson concentrated on manufacturing cheesemaking technology and marketing his

The Cheese King of Glengarry County, D.M. MacPherson.

MacPherson family photographed beside the Allengrove Cheese Factory, Lancaster, Ontario.

Cheese box factory,
Maberly, Ontario.

cheese, using an office in Montreal to sell directly to English importers. But markets faltered during the recession of the late 1800s and, in 1903, the Allengrove combine collapsed.[27]

The joint-stock company was a variation on the cooperative milk pools run by the earliest commercial cheesemakers such as Ballantyne and Farrington but with the farmers owning the factory and thus controlling the whole operation. This became the dominant form of factory organization through the central part of the province, where wealth was perhaps most evenly spread among the farmers of the district, with few having a great deal of money to spare. It built on the tradition of bees and doing things "on shares." By spreading the risk across a number of farmer-shareholders, it created a stability that sustained these factories through the many downs and outs of depending on the English export market and the English merchants.

In Lanark County, the minutes of a meeting held December 1, 1883, detail the founding of a cheese-factory cooperative at Hopetown:

Moved by John Taylor, sec. by Chs. McIlraith, that we bind ourselves to furnish at least the number of cows opposite our names for the term of six years. Carried.

Moved by John Stewart, sec'd by Thos. Bullock Sen. that the factory be built by the patrons and by any others who wish to take stock in the company. Carried.

Moved by Stewart Baird, sec'd. by Findly Gunn that the lowest shares be $10. Carried.

Moved by Steward Baird, sec'd. by Thomas Pretty that these proceedings be null and void if cows enough are not obtained."[28]

Seventy-eight shares were sold, and the milk of 147 cows promised. The cheese factory went ahead.

The cooperatives were managed by the farmer-shareholders, who in turn governed their affairs through a series of by-laws passed at the annual meetings. At St. Mary's in Perth County, the by-laws of the Blanshard and Nissouri factory covered more than a dozen pages. By-law 7 required that milk be delivered to the factory in tin pails, not in wooden buckets or the tanks which farmers used for hauling water and sap from the maple bush in the spring. By-law 10 stipulated that the milk drawer was not to start picking up farmers' milk before 6 o'clock in the morning or to drive too fast. In yet another by-law that comments on the state of rural roads, the man drawing in the milk was held accountable for any that spilled along the way.

At Atwood, the Elma Cheese and Butter Co. (later, the Atwood Cheese Factory) had no less than 20 rules just for the milk haulers. One specified that "no milk drawer shall drive faster than at the rate of three miles per hour, exclusive of the time of putting on or taking off the cans, and he shall not leave any milk-stand until the regular time for leaving the stand."[29] The stand was a wooden platform, sometimes with a lean-to roof, where farmers left their milk cans in the morning and received them back later, sometimes filled with whey.

Many factories used tenders and auctions for everything from hauling the milk to disposing of whey to acquiring ice (for cooling the curing room), as well as cheese boxes and other supplies, and even for building the cheese factory and engaging a cheesemaker for the season. Doing as much as possible by barter and trade within the local economy, they kept their cash requirements to a minimum — an inclination which the historic lack of money in the rural regions made almost instinctive.

In Prince Edward County, the farmers who founded the Cherry Valley Cheese Factory in 1868 had to take out a loan. Understandably, therefore, they kept their capital requirements to a minimum. First, having canvassed the district for a spot with a plentiful supply of fresh water, which is vital both for cooling curds and cleaning cheese-factory equipment, they negotiated to buy some land by a spring from one of its shareholders, for $50 plus all the manure made by the hogs they'd be keeping there. They then organized a bee for drawing in stone for the foundation, though they hired a carpenter to build the factory itself. Issuing a tender for cheesemaking, they accepted an offer by Jacob Collier to make cheese for $75 a month. They

Excerpt from D.M. M^{ac}Pherson's Diary:

MARCH 29, 1872: Made cheese. 94 lbs. Set at 78 (degrees) Curd came in 15 minues. Cut in one hour. Used new knives, worked well. Cut three times. Curd had a good flavour. Acid came very strongly. Passed in curd mill and then salted. The whey did not appear to press out well. Took out and broke it up, then pressed again. Added a bit more salt.[31]

then organized four milk-hauling routes, each covering a milkshed (akin to a watershed) extending little more than three miles from the factory but including up to 15 shareholders and the milk of up to 100 cows. They organized a public auction for tendering the hauling work, which paid roughly a dollar a day for a seasonal total of about $100. For the work and the hardship involved, it wasn't much remuneration, and few of the farmers and local craftsmen (one was a tailor, one was a shoemaker) who took it up carried on for more than a season.

Though many factories sent whey home to farmers, many others arranged to keep pigs at the factory. At Cherry Valley, shareholders sent their pigs to the factory where they were fattened on the whey through the season and often sold together at the end of it. The tie-in between hogs and cheesemaking was common and provided a much-needed ballast in times of low cheese prices. In fact, while hog sales were often earmarked for paying the taxes and cheese sales earmarked for the mortgage, in some years it was reversed, with the proceeds from cheese paying the taxes and pork sales paying the mortgage.[30]

Cheese Mammoths and Their Champions

The businessmen of Ingersoll made it a point to read the local paper. When they learned about Harvey Farrington's booming little cheese factory outside of Norwich, they decided to pay him a visit.

The delegation was led by Charles Chadwick, manager of the local Niagara District Bank, agent for Canada Permanent Building and Savings Society plus three insurance companies, and president of the Ingersoll Agricultural Society. He was accompanied by Adam Olliver, who ran a lumber mill (which would soon turn out cheese boxes) and served as the Mayor of Ingersoll, as well as James Noxon, foundryman and implement maker (who would soon produce

cheesemaking equipment) and Daniel Phaelan, listed in the *Ingersoll Who's Who* simply as a "capitalist." The businessmen were in turn accompanied by two farmers considering a move into commercial cheesemaking, James Harris and George Galloway, along with cheesemaker Robert Facey from the Ranney establishment. Galloway's cheesemaker at the time was James Crawford. Recording the visit later, Crawford noted that the businessmen "took plenty of time to inspect every particular of Mr. Farrington's new venture. They decided that cheesemaking on the factory system was going to be a paying branch of farm husbandry for the farmers of Canada, and were all delighted

Top: Manotick Cheese
Factory, circa 1895.

Bottom: The first cheese
factory in Carleton County,
North Gower, Ontario,
circa 1870.

beyond measure with their visit with Mr. Farrington who treated them very cordially."

They were so delighted that they soon regrouped at the offices of the Niagara District Bank, with Charles Chadwick presiding. In addition to the gentlemen who'd visited Farrington's plant, there were Edwin Casswell, a cheese exporter, Charles Wilson, and Harvey Farrington himself. (Thomas Ballantyne of Stratford and D. Derbyshire of Brockville sent their regrets but also their consent to the propositions to be discussed at the meeting.)

There were two propositions on the agenda: the formation of a provincial marketing association; and the manufacture of a mammoth cheese as a promotional device for the province's cheese. As Mr. Chadwick reportedly told the meeting: "Trade could not be conducted on a local, or parochial, scale."[1]

The tradition of making mammoths was hardly new. However, it had reached new proportions in 1840 when cheesemakers in the Cheddar district of England prepared a mammoth measuring 20 feet in height and nine feet in girth as a wedding present for Queen Victoria. History does not record the Queen's reaction, if politeness did not stifle it at the time. Whatever its initial reception, the cheese came to be known as "England's Monster."

Still, it was known, and as advertisers will attest, that's what counts. But timing is vital too: being first with a new idea, not second.

Therein lay a potential problem. While Harris and other local cheesemakers were planning their mammoth, Andes Smith was already at work on his own.

Smith had been operating a farm-based cheese factory since at least 1861, entirely as a private concern. He took in milk "from all comers," paying six cents a hundredweight and even hauling it with his own wagons and teamsters.[2] The 1861 agricultural census reported 14,000 pounds of cheese produced on his farm, with a further 15,000 pounds reported on the farm next door, owned by Henry Smith. In the summer of 1865, he was said to be doing "the largest business of any factory yet started in Canada." In its August 1 edition, the *Canada Farmer* also reported that Smith had "a mammoth cheese in a press constructed for its especial accommodation, which is intended to eclipse all the cheeses ever manufactured either in the old world or the new." The finished cheese was five feet in diameter, three feet high, and weighed about 4,000 pounds. It was to be exhibited at the Provincial Exhibition, according to the newspaper, "and we notify our readers to look out for the monster cheese. Our friend Ranney will we fear lose his laurels unless he is quietly at work making a cheese a little bigger than the one just described."[3]

The Smith cheese mammoth won first prize at the Utica Fair in New York, where it was hauled onto the exhibition grounds by 10 yoke of oxen festooned in maple leaves. Back in Canada, a four-horse team prepared to haul it to the Provincial Exhibition at London. But somehow the wagon overturned, the cheese fell out, was broken apart and destroyed.[4]

Months later, the Americans had abrogated the free-trade Reciprocity Treaty, stifling grain and cattle exports to the American market and prompting more farmers to switch to cheese-making. As well, with the Civil War over, American cheese merchants were moving to regain their position in the English market. Both factors augured a collapse of the cheese business in Canada West before it could fully establish itself. Now was the time for collective effort. Time for the Ingersoll Mammoth.

A private corporation, called the Ingersoll Cheese Company, had been formed to sponsor the project and, incidentally, to export its share-holders' cheese. James Harris, Harvey Farrington, George Galloway, Robert Facey, and Charles Wilson were listed among the shareholders. They could guarantee both the necessary milk and knowledgeable cheesemakers for the mammoth. James Noxon, the implement dealer whose "spirit and enterprise" had been fulsomely praised by the local paper when he brought out a new line of reapers and mowers in 1864, was chairman of the board.[5] Charles Chadwick was secretary, and Edwin Caswell was listed as company salesman. By the time the Ingersoll Mammoth left Ingersoll on its mini world tour in the

Charles Chadwick, Secretary of the Ingersoll Cheese Company.

Robert Facey, Head Cheesemaker, Ingersoll Mammoth.

James Crawford,
Cheesemaker for
Harvey Farrington.

Daniel Derbyshire,
President of the Eastern
Ontario Dairymen's
Association.

fall of 1866, Caswell had shipped over 4,000 boxes (180 tons) of cheese directly to England.

The milk from 2,400 cows of some 250 farmers was used in making the cheese in June 1866. Robert Facey served as head cheesemaker, supervising his own assistant at the Harris factories, his replacement at the Ranneys, and the cheesemaker working for George Galloway. These were Miles Harris, Warren Schell, and James Crawford.[6]

These makers stayed in their own factories working up the milk into cheese and pressing the curd for 48 hours in their own winch-screw presses. Then they trucked the cheese hoops over to the main Harris factory, ingeniously positioned opposite the tollgate along the roadway (what is now Highway 19) so that patrons of the factory, by entering the driveways on either side, could avoid paying the toll.[7] In a 16-foot-square lean-to constructed specially for the mammoth, Robert Facey supervised the work of putting the partly pressed curd through the curd mill, then salting it and shovelling it into a giant steel hoop supplied by James Noxon. When this was filled and the follower inserted, the curds were pressed for eight days under the pressure of four jack screws turned with iron shafts. Once out of the press, the cheese was swathed in 45 yards of cloth, then wrapped in a special bandage of galvanized wire screen to help maintain the cheese's posture, while still allowing it to breathe throughout the curing process. To help turn the cheese every day or two, which is also essential for proper aging, Noxon and a Mr. C.P. Hall devised a swinging frame in which they set the cheese for aging. A hoop placed around the cheese held it within the frame. Bolts from there to the side of the frame acted as a pivot, while bolts at either end could be removed so that the cheese could be rotated with a simple push of the hand.[8]

When it was time to ship the mammoth, they had to dismantle one wall of the lean-to in order to load it into an iron cheese box. This increased the weight from 7,300 pounds to 8,000 pounds — an even four tons. A crowd of helpers then rolled the cheese box onto a lumber wagon donated by the Sweaburg Sawmill and constructed especially not only to support the load but to maximize the sense of its six-foot-ten-inch diameter and three feet of height. With three teams of powerful dapple-grey Percherons to haul it, the Ingersoll Mammoth, its creators, and a growing crowd of its admirers set off up the road for the Great Western Railway Station. Young Miles Harris walked unobtrusively beside the wagon carrying a mallet because one of the wagon wheels was in danger of falling off. As he walked along, he whacked the hub cap periodically with his mallet, happily forestalling the fate of the Andes Smith mammoth, which has virtually disappeared from the historical record.[9]

The cheese's departure from the Ingersoll railway station duly made it onto the pages of

Top: Ingersoll Cheese Mammoth on tour in Saratoga, New York, with James Harris shown right of the wagon and on the left Charles Chadwick and Hiram and Lydia Chase Ranney (just visible behind her husband's right shoulder), 1866.

Bottom: Canada's second cheese mammoth, made in Perth, Ontario, on display at the Chicago World's Fair, 1893.

The Story of Ontario Cheddar Cheese ❧ 49

the *Ingersoll Chronicle*, 7 September, 1866:

An unusual excitement was created amongst our citizens last evening by the removal of the Mammoth Cheese, preceded by the Ingersoll Brass Band to the Railway Station to be shipped to the New York State Fair which is to be held next week at Saratoga.

A large number of our townspeople collected at the station to signify their appreciation of the spirit and enterprise displayed by the proprietors of the Ingersoll Cheese Factory in producing from their extensive establishment the largest cheese ever known to be made. Appropriate speeches were made by Messrs. Chadwick, Noxon, Harris, Blackman and Gibson and the occasion was made a very agreeable and pleasant one.[10]

There is no record of the cheese having won top honours for its texture and flavour at the Saratoga Fair, nor at the Provincial Exhibition before it was shipped to England. There were rumours that the Ingersoll Mammoth had been denied anchorage when it arrived in Liverpool on account of its noxious odour and seeping, deteriorated condition, and that it virtually had to be smuggled into the country by the salesman, James Caswell; however, these stories were thought to have originated from rivals in the by-then highly competitive cheese market. James Crawford penned an unblemished account, describing the English tour as a happy round of parades and exhibits in parks, with Messrs. Harris and Phaelan (and doubtless also Caswell, though he isn't mentioned) in attendance at them all. From what Crawford understood,

the arrival of the cheese in the English market caused a great sensation among the cheese and other merchants, all of whom were highly pleased, and praised the enterprise of the Canadian people in taking this method of establishing a wholesale trade between England and Canada. . . . The shipping of the mammoth cheese to England was without doubt the greatest advertisement for colonial product that it had ever received on the British market up to that time.[11]

Almost overnight, Ontario cheddar became an export staple, with a name in the English market that would endure for over a century.

The Ingersoll Mammoth became a symbol of that promotional triumph, certainly in the eyes of Ontario's cheese poet, James McIntrye. McIntrye penned one of his more tortured poems in honour of the mammoth cheese. It's the one for which he is perhaps most famous.

Ode on the Mammoth Cheese

(Weighing over 7,000 pounds)

We have seen thee Queen of cheese,
Laying quietly at your ease,
Gently fanned by evening breeze —
Thy fair form no flies dare seize.

All gaily dressed soon you'll go
To the great Provincial Show,
To be admired by many a beau
in the City of Toronto.

Cows numerous as a swarm of bees —
Or as leaves upon the trees —
It did require to make thee please,
And stand unrivalled Queen of Cheese.

May you not receive a scar as!
We have heard that Mr. Harris
Intends to send you off as far as
The great World's show at Paris.
Of the youth — beware of these —
For some of them might rudely squeeze
And bite your cheek; then songs or glees
We could not sing o' Queen of Cheese.

We'rt thou suspended from baloon
You'd caste a shade, even at noon;
Folks would think it was the moon
About to fall and crush them soon.[12]

This ode is not the only totem of Ontario cheddar. There is also the world's only monument to cheese: a concrete replica of the 11-ton 1893 mammoth cheese, located on the outskirts of Perth, Ontario. According to a latter-day report in the local paper, "Foreigners have been known to mistake it for a launching pad for guided missiles."[13] Canadians, one assumes, think in different symbolic terms.

While the Ingersoll Mammoth was the initiative of cheesemakers themselves and, initially at least, for the benefit of everyone in the industry, the mammoth at Perth was largely a government initiative. It was sponsored by Canada's first Dairy Commissioner, James Robertson, although partly, it seems, through the initiative of a couple of the early cheesemaking entrepreneurs who were also involved in government. One was Daniel Derbyshire, the legislative representative (MPP) for Brockville.[14] This might be the same individual who in 1865 had been unable to attend the Ingersoll meeting chaired by Charles Chadwick to discuss a possible provincial marketing association and the Ingersoll cheese mammoth. Some of the credit is also attributed to D.M. MacPherson, who at the time was the local candidate for the farmer-reformers called the Patrons of Industry.[15]

Alternately known as "Canada's Monster Cheese," the "Canadian Mite" and, in Quebec as "Fromage Elephant," the "Mammoth Cheese from Canada" (as it was officially called) was made in much the same way as the Ingersoll Mammoth. But at 22,000 pounds (compared to 7,000 in the Ingersoll model), the scale was huge. Twelve cheesemakers and 12 factories, working under the supervision of James Ruddick, assisted by George Publow, were involved in the initial stages of making up the milk into curd. Once they had cheddared the cheese and cut it into curds, they loaded these into milk cans and hauled them to the Canadian Pacific Railway freight shed at Perth where a special press had been constructed, possibly by D.M. MacPherson. Made of quarter-inch boiler plate and measuring nine feet across and six feet high, the press itself weighed 3,000 pounds. Here Ruddick, who was with the federal government's experimental station at Perth, and Publow, who was a travelling cheesemaking instructor with the Ontario government, organized the loading and pressing of the curds.

It took three days' worth of cheese curds from all 12 factories — or an estimated 207,200 pounds of milk — to fill the press. Then the cover was placed inside, and the 12 screw presses were set to work. The cheese was cured over the winter, while final promotional plans went forward. A special flatbed truck was built for transporting the cheese on its promotional tour of England, and permission obtained from the London authorities to pull such monstrous tonnage through the city's venerable streets. But first, the cheese was to go to the great Chicago World's Fair in 1893.

It travelled by train from Perth through Toronto to Windsor, en route to Chicago. It was laid out in beribboned splendour on an open flat car, followed by a second car carrying the special display wagon and four 1,000-pound mini-mammoths donated by D.M. MacPherson. The railway prepared a special poster detailing the cheese's tour through Ontario and inviting the public to visit it along the way.

It drew a crowd of 5,000 at the station in North Toronto and, by the time it arrived in Chicago, it had been so completely autographed that its entire surface was smothered in names. Its casing was then cleaned and repainted before the cheese was trucked onto the fairgrounds. It was duly installed — then crashed through the flooring of the display hall, winning it instant notoriety for the duration of the fair.

The *Chicago Tribune* reported that "the Mammoth Cheese from Canada is attracting more attention and comment than perhaps any other single exhibition in any department on the grounds. It is surrounded by visitors from morning till night." Not only did the mammoth score a 95 out of 100 when it was entered in competition. Of the 849 entries of Canadian cheese at the fair, 736 of them were awarded medals or diplomas. Canadian cheesemakers won 103 prizes for cheese made previous to 1893 (while Americans won none), and Canadians won 369 awards (compared with 45 for Americans) for cheese made that year.[16] At least one of those prizes went to a woman, Annie Elevier of Madoc. Another went to Alex MacLaren, whose cheese scored the only perfect score during the fair.[17]

The English tour was organized by Arthur Rowson, a cheese importer from Tooley Street in London, who sold the cheese to the London caterer, Jubal Webb. Together they organized a parade of the mammoth through downtown London and installed it in a special exhibition hall festooned with flags and evergreens in the West End. Ladders were erected to allow personal inspection of the cheese. Samples were cut with garden spades. Sir Charles Tupper represented the Canadian Government in a special tasting ceremony, and a sample was sent home to James Robertson. He in turn circulated samples to the House of Commons, the Senate, and the Press Gallery. And for a moment, everyone knew about Canadian cheddar cheese.

But a moment is not enough. Periodic promotional efforts are not enough. What was needed, and called for from the beginning, was a collective marketing organization to champion the economic interests of Ontario cheddar and defend them against the powerful interests of the English mercantile elite, here represented by cheese importers. The Ontario Dairymen's Association was to have been this organization.

The Canadian Dairymen's Association

The companies that imported Ontario cheddar to England dated back to when the old walled cities like London functioned almost as city states. The Lord Mayor issued licences for certain companies or guilds to operate within the protection of the city's walls and held them accountable for setting standards, weights, and measures as well as for policing their members. The cheesemongers belonged to the company of grocers or food merchants. They imported cheeses from the English countryside and sold them in the old covered markets such as Fleete Market near the Fleete River (described as "an open sewer"), as well as Newgate and Covent Garden.[1]

In the mid-1700s, a yeoman's son from Essex, James Fitch, was apprenticed to a freeman in the company of grocers in London. By 1859, the firm Fitch and Son was a thriving grocery business in its own right, with advertisements quoting one satisfied customer located at a mission in Zambezi, Africa, a Dr. David Livingstone. Dr. Livingstone wrote glowingly to Mr. Fitch that "the hams you sent kept admirably; the bacon too was in good condition."[2] Increasingly, Fitch acquired his cured pork, as well as cheese and other produce which kept well in an age before refrigeration, not from the English countryside but from the colonies of British North America where supplies were cheaper.

As England expanded its empire, farmers, mallsters, and cheesemakers in the countryside were displaced by competition from the colonies. Those who could adjust upward did so by moving into the cities as these burst their feudal walls and became commercial centres in the mercantile stage of capitalism. There they became commercial agents themselves, importing cheese, whisky, flour, and other foodstuffs from farmers in the colonies and selling these in the local markets and, later, to the industrializing north.

At the time of Messrs. Harris and Phaelan's tour with the Ingersoll Mammoth, the firms were still small, family partnerships like Fitch and Son and Lovell and Christmas. William Lovell's story was almost identical to that of James Fitch. He, too, had left the family farm in Somerset to enter the cheesemongering trade in London in the 1840s. One of his daughters, Mary Cary, married Josiah Christmas, who formed the Lovell and Christmas cheese and produce trading partnership with Mary's brother William.[3]

It's possible that James Harris, Daniel Phaelan, and Edwin Caswell, or some of the other emerging Ontario cheese entrepreneurs — Thomas Ballantyne of Stratford, Daniel Derbyshire of Brockville, and D.M. MacPherson

of Lancaster, for example — would have welcomed a partnership with one of those established London firms. But in empires, power tends to be concentrated at the centre. Colonies are kept on the margins, are kept subordinate and, if possible, dependent on the metropolitan imperial centres. The pattern asserted itself here with seemingly ineluctable momentum, although there were choices involved.

One of the choices was over the formation of collective industrial associations. One option was a local, quasi-national solidarity between the producers of cheese and the local companies involved in marketing it to the British importers; another was a more class-like solidarity between local cheese merchants and those in England. The Canadian Dairymen's Association could have become a local counterweight to the importers' clout if the choice had favoured local solidarity. Harvey Farrington, one of the movers behind its formation, wanted it modelled after the American Dairymen's Association, a federation of county associations. The Herkimer County Dairymen's Association, of which Farrington was the first financial agent, was formed (in 1845) "for the purpose of marketing cheese more equitably and directly, and without the aid and expense of local buyers or middlemen."[4] Ensuring a uniform high standard in cheesemaking among the 100 or so members of the association was a related consideration.

In January 1866, Farrington persuaded

James Harris and Charles Chadwick to accompany him to New York for the annual meeting of the American Dairymen's Association. Curiously though, nothing was done until July the following year, after the Ingersoll Mammoth project, sponsored by the Ingersoll Cheese Company, which was owned by commercial shareholders from Oxford County.

On a pleasant July day that year of Canada's creation as a nation-state, upwards of 200 dairymen (cheesemakers and interested businessmen) gathered in the red-brick splendour of the Ingersoll Town Hall, their transportation having been thoughtfully donated by the railway. There, they passed a founding resolution, dedicating themselves to "mutual improvement in the science of cheesemaking and more efficient action in promoting the general interests of the dairy community."[5]

The marketing idea had been sidelined. Marketing, and all the power issues it entailed, was left to small private companies like the Ingersoll Cheese Company and Thomas Ballantyne and Sons in neighbouring Perth County, and to the already powerful network of British produce and forwarding merchants all centred in and loyal to London and, to a lesser extent, Glasgow and Liverpool. The dairymen's association, which would shortly split into the dairymen's associations of Western and Eastern Ontario, concentrated on supplying the best cheese possible for the various merchants.

The Honorable Thomas Ballantyne, Speaker of the Ontario Legislature and founding Vice-President of the Canadian Dairymen's Association.

Ingersoll Town Hall, site of the founding of the Canadian Dairymen's Association in 1867.

Certainly, cultivating consistent and high standards was important. The industry was growing fast, demanding more cheesemakers than there were qualified men available. For instance, when Jacob Collier was hired as cheesemaker at the Cherry Valley cheese factory in Prince Edward County in 1867, the county directory had him listed as a labourer. Women were being phased out of cheesemaking at this time, although many were hired as cheesemaking assistants and some travelled from plant to plant "to serve as spare cheesemaker when needed. This service was appreciated since they were neater, tidier and more careful. The final cheese quality was usually very good."[6]

The dairymen's association functioned a lot like the old craft guilds — instructing and disciplining its members, setting and enforcing standards. In one of its first initiatives outside its own sphere of influence, it drafted legislation making the adulteration of milk a punishable offence. Unfortunately, this law was later ruled *ultra vires*, with regulation of milk deemed a federal matter. Adulterating milk, either by skimming off cream or adding water, was an ongoing problem, taking up cheesemakers' and factory-inspectors' time testing milk with lactometers and the Babcock test and trying to discipline offenders.

From the beginning, the dairymen's association supported good cheese and cheesemaking with instruction. The first annual meeting of the dairymen's association in 1868 featured Mr. X.A. Willard of Utica, New York, who lectured on sanitary procedures and scientific methods for making quality cheese. James Noxon also spoke on the subject of cleanliness, augmenting this with advice to pay what was required to outfit a successful factory and noting that he manufactured all "the machinery and instruments necessary for the manufacture of cheese."[7] Harvey Farrington was another regular guest speaker until his death in 1878, giving generous advice on the proper making of sweet-tasting cheese. At his death, the association engaged the services of Professor L.B. Arnold of New York to act as itinerant instructor. When the association didn't rehire him the following year, Thomas Ballantyne (then Speaker of the Ontario Legislature) filled the gap, paying for an itinerant instructor out of his own pocket as a service to the dairying community.[8] By 1880, the Dairymen's Association of Western Ontario had hired four master cheesemakers as itinerant instructors and factory inspectors. They were paid in part by the association, partly by a $10 annual levy on factories wanting this service, and partly by a provincial subsidy.[9]

Every year, the instructor-inspectors reported back to the dairymen's annual meetings. It seems that most factories were kept fairly well. For instance, in 1892, one inspector evaluated 11 factories as "clean," three as "fair," and only two as "dirty." The latter, however, were very bad, with "floors and gutters leaking . . . a pool of rotten whey under the factory . . . and a cess-pool" in the yard behind it.[10]

Instruction improved, with the association opening a summer dairy school at Tavistock in Western Ontario in 1891.[11] It opened a second one in Eastern Ontario a year later, thanks to a $750 annual provincial subsidy.[12] Sanitary standards in the plants didn't rise accordingly, however, partly because their application hinged on a larger problem related to marketing. As one account put it, "since the price of cheese fluctuated, cheesemakers were not always able to employ additional help to clean the factory or its utensils."

And as one of the instructors reported in 1902:

the sanitary condition at many factories is very poor, there being leaking floors and leaking gutters. In some places we find no drainage at all, and in some places where there is drainage, it is completely blocked up.

There are still a number of makers who keep their vats, presses and pails covered with that natural paint, dirt. In some places, it is not safe to touch anything unless you want to stick there.[13]

That same year, the provincial government intervened more actively, appointing George Barr as

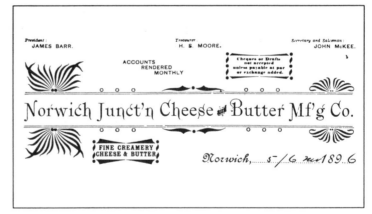

Top: Advertisement for the West Zorra Cheese Factory in *The Atlas of Oxford County*, 1876.

Bottom: Letterhead for Norwich Junction Cheese and Butter Mfg. Co., 1896.

chief dairy instructor for Western Ontario and George Publow as chief instructor for Eastern Ontario. This marked the beginning of the Dairy Branch of the Ontario Department of Agriculture, although it wasn't formally established until 1904. As well, the pre-eminence of the dairymen's association as industry regulator was preserved for some additional years by the fact that, for instance, George Barr and his successor, Frank Herns, served simultaneously on the executive of the dairymen's association.

Gradually, the Dairy Branch assumed more responsibility and control. It opened a provincial dairy school at the Ontario Agricultural College in Guelph in 1893, which was open to women as well as men.[14] Starting in 1892, it also sent out "travelling dairies," which set up shop at county and township fairs and were very popular.[15] An Eastern Dairy School was opened in Kingston in 1894, and a satellite Western Dairy School opened at Strathroy in 1896. Dairy instructors explained the science of cheesemaking and the importance of sanitation. They also explained the new technologies emerging with the steam phase of mechanization, then electrification and, later, computerization and automation. For instance, when steam power launched the first phase of mass production, it prompted a new wave of inventions applying steam power to cheesemaking. In Hastings County, J.C. Brintnell adapted the curd rake and paddle to mechanized motion and invented the power agitator.[16] Steam-powered technologies, augmenting the original hand-powered implements fashioned in farm dairies, became the standard in Ontario cheese factories until well into the 1940s and 1950s.

In 1906, the province appointed sanitary inspectors and the entire system of instruction and inspection came under the official direction of the Agriculture Department.[17] Government and the dairymen's associations continued working closely together, however, buttressing a commitment to quality craftsmanship. In 1911, for instance, the Dairy Branch began classifying and licensing cheesemakers in response to lobbying by the dairymen for enforceable professional standards.

The Ontario Agricultural College also served as a research lab for Ontario dairymen. In 1897, it checked out the workings of some of the early models of milking machines and found them "difficult to clean."[18] A year later, it investigated an outbreak of "billy goat flavour" or, as it was also described, "goose flavour" in the cheese being made in Middlesex and Huron Counties. It experimented with pepsin versus rennet for coagulating cheese milk, tested different temperatures for aging and storing cheese, and found that "block" cheese didn't breathe as well as the traditional cylinder shape in storage. The college also published bulletins outlining its research findings and other developments in the industry.

Loading cheese boxes on board the *Belleville* at Belleville, Ontario.

Top: Alex MacLaren, cheese exporter.

Bottom: Loading cheese into a ship's hold for international export.

By the early 1900s, the pattern of the industry was set. The marketing issue had been sidelined, but there was at least broad institutional support for making quality cheddar cheese across the province. Cheesemaking, grossing about $10 million a year,[19] had become the third-ranked industry in all Ontario.[20] In 1904, Canada exported 234 million pounds of cheddar cheese, almost all of it to Britain, where it had installed itself as a staple in the factory worker's diet.

On the downside, the beginning of a dark unravelling thread, the Ingersoll Cheese Company was quietly taken over by a British importing firm. In nearby Stratford, Thomas Ballantyne and Sons continued into the next generation as a modestly successful family firm. Meanwhile, the British importers Lovell and Christmas merged with the Fitch family firm to form Fitch-Lovell and Christmas with branch offices in Australia, New Zealand, and Canada; in 1901, one of Thomas Ballantyne's sons, Robert, accepted a position in their Montreal office as "managing director for Canada." The Ballantyne firm faded from the scene. Finally, there was Alex MacLaren, who'd worked for the Ballantynes before launching his own export firm. Through the early 1900s, he expanded it internationally, opening offices in England and on the Continent. The trend in Canadian business under the National Policy, however, had become one of diversification — otherwise known as integration — through mergers with British or American firms. MacLaren relocated to Toronto and broadened his holdings with minority interests in a wood veneer company, an American cement company, and some American insurance companies.[21] In the early 1920s, he sold out his cheese business to a budding entrepreneur from Chicago, James Kraft.[22]

Still, the effects of this unravelling were slow to be seen or acted upon. With 1,233 factories across the province, Ontario cheddar was a major factor moving Ontario farms from a subsistence to a money economy.[23] At the turn of the century, it had fulfilled the promise of James McIntyre's symbolic poetry and become a major Ontario institution, seemingly as eternal as the church. Every season for nearly a hundred years, the cheese factories produced their cheese, which was shipped to Montreal and from there to England, where it yielded steady if modest returns to farmers and cheesemakers across the province.

PART TWO

"When
the Cheese
Money Paid
the Mortgage"

Union Star Cheese Factory
Renfrew, Ontario

Prologue

The twitter of barnswallows snips the flanneled stillness of pre-dawn. The rooster crows; another answers from the neighbours' farm. Lilac drifts in at the open window.

Downstairs, there's a shudder of iron as the ashes are shaken through the grate of the black wood stove, the scrape of the ash box being pushed back inside. Then a soft rustle of paper being scrunched, kindling being thatched over top, and finally a clunk as the cast-iron lid is set back in place over the firebox. The day's fire is set and ready to light. Silence, then Father calls for the boys, and it's milking time.

Growing up on a farm just outside Sheatown, Claude Flood was 10 when he started driving the family's milk to the local cheese factory in 1908.

"It was about a mile and a half. The neighbour boy, he used to go too, and we used to race the horses." A chuckle. "The butterfat wasn't so high in them days."[1]

Over the hill at Forfar, Talmage Stone was also 10 when he was given the job.

"Well, the old mare, she knew where to go and what to do, and I kind of come along with her. And there'd always be some old man; you'd run by him if you could, though he didn't like that very well."[2]

Passing a neighbour also meant getting ahead in the line-up at the factory as milk came in from individual farmers or through teamsters hauling from the milksheds fanning out from the factory. In the days before refrigeration — which lasted into the 1930s and 1940s in some districts — five miles was about the outer limit for hauling, which kept factories fairly small.

Lack of money kept things small too, because the banks were geared to commercial trade rather than industrial development, and deposits habitually exceeded local borrowings.[3] In the cities and large towns, however, the scale of manufacturing steadily increased as mechanization moved beyond the clumsiness of steam to the greater efficiency of internal combustion, of which the Americans were the principle pioneers. Not surprisingly, therefore, this increasing scale of industrialization often took the form of American foreign investment. This sometimes occurred through partnerships and mergers, such as the McLaughlin-Buick motor car company, formed in 1907.

Robert McLaughlin of Oshawa, whose carriageworks dated back to the 1870s and whose business spanned the British Empire, supplied the body for the horseless carriage, while David Buick of Detroit supplied the engines. Eventually McLaughlin's sons sold out their portion of the business, which became General Motors in 1918.[4]

Increasingly, however, foreign investment took the form of branch plants, built under the protective umbrella of Canada's National Policy. Many of these were in the dairy business, including the Borden Company of New Jersey. In 1908, its condensed milk plants at Tillsonburg and Ingersoll were valued at between $100,000 and $150,000.[5] Ten years later, it was considered big news that a new cheddar cheese factory was built nearby at a cost of $3,500.[6] Even into the 1930s, the average cheese factory was valued at only $4,000, including land, building, and equipment.[7] The scale remained very small.

Mergers and combines not only increased the scale of operations. They also consolidated power and centralized operations into fewer, larger urban centres. The Grand Trunk Railway and Great Western merged in the early 1880s, virtually eliminating competition throughout Ontario. Where there were 54 textile factories in 1885, by 1891 there were only 17, with the two biggest controlling 70 per cent of production.[8] Where there were 51 banks in Canada in 1874, there were only eleven by 1925. Of the 36 banks to disappear since 1900, 27 were involved in mergers.[9]

This was a crucial consolidation, for it served to centralize further development away from small rural centres into a few major cities. As one example, local efforts to start a cannery in small-town Glencoe failed when the local bank manager refused to finance local business people. Yet the same bank approved a loan for the branch plant of a Toronto firm. It even drew on Glencoe citizens' local deposits to supply the funds.[10]

The consolidations laid the groundwork for the second phase of mechanized mass production through the electrification of factories. This increased the scale of manufacturing, creating more job opportunities in the manufacturing centres. In turn, as more people (mostly immigrants) entered the factory labour force, they consolidated the cities as the power centres of a modern industrialized Ontario.

Ontario's population, which had been 81 per cent rural in 1871, was only 57 per cent rural by 1901.[11] By 1921, Ontario's population was 58 per cent urban, the same year Edison Electric built a Canadian General Electric plant in Peterborough, ushering in the complement to mechanized mass production — namely, mass consumption, involving consumer products such as electric toasters, ovens, and fridges.[12] Guelph, Galt, Berlin (Kitchener), Stratford, Chatham, Woodstock, and St. Thomas evolved from agricultural centres to manufacturing centres as they reoriented their production from farm implements to household appliances.

Ontario's transformation from agricultural heartland to industrial heartland meant relative neglect for the people living in the countryside,

Farmers delivering milk to the factory line up to unload.

especially for the poorer regions in the Eastern counties. Oliver Mowat, who served as Premier of Ontario from 1872 to 1896, contributed considerably to this neglect. He came into office as a champion of rural Ontario, establishing a provincial department of agriculture and expanding grants to agricultural societies;[13] however, his attention soon shifted to resource industries and manufacturing. These became his foundation for a mini "Empire Ontario," with the northwest of the province, and later the Prairies, treated as resource hinterland to south-central Ontario's industrial metropolitan centres.

The urban population was the main beneficiary of this policy thrust. City people enjoyed better public hygiene and transportation facilities, better education and other social services. While out in the countryside, farmers, cheesemakers, and other craft-scale workers felt abandoned, even betrayed. An 1896 report noted that most rural roads were still "little better than trails" and "practically impassable for at least two months of the year."[14] In fact, poor roads became the second biggest cost in cheddar cheese making and a gnawing factor contributing to the industry's decline.[15]

Schooling was about as bad as the roads. First, there were no high schools in the country, only in cities and large towns. Then, what little schooling existed was badly underfunded. An 1898 report by the National Council of Women found that rural school teachers were paid less than half what teachers were paid in the cities. Poor education left some cheesemakers illiterate, even into the 1950s, and shied them away from dairy schools run by the province. They relied instead on apprenticeships with master cheesemakers, monthly meetings of county cheesemakers' associations, and the annual dairymen's association meetings, plus helpful visits from the itinerant cheese-factory instructors such as Frank Herns and his successor, Jack Bain. The oral tradition of learning, which survived with the craft associations, helped sustain Ontario cheddar right to the end.

Nothing, however, could make up for the chronic lack of political and economic support. The National Policy hurt the farming community. The defeat of free trade in the election of 1911 cut farmers off from ready access to the U.S. market for their produce. Furthermore, from the earliest days of protectionism, they'd been forced to pay higher prices for locally manufactured goods produced by domestic (often branch-plant) suppliers protected by the National Policy's high import tariffs.

Walter Riddell, who served as Northumberland County Reeve during this period, penned an angry paper against protectionism, which he never presented to the local agricultural society. In it, he railed against what he called the "extortion" of protective tariffs and high local prices charged by the so-called "infant manufacturers" of the day.

He began the paper in a manner reminiscent of William Lyon MacKenzie's Reform vision, by naming agriculture as the foundation of all economy:

Agriculture, as it is the most ancient, is also the most important, and most useful worldly pursuit; the more agriculture flourishes, the more will commerce, manufactures, the arts and sciences flourish. There is no useful calling that does not receive benefit from the prosperity of agriculture. . . . Destroy it and you bring in one common grave, national power and individual prosperity.

After a lengthy discourse on the natural elements afflicting farmers, such as the weather, Riddell then went on to the man-made ones:

Another hindrance to agriculture is that the farmers are taxed to support, or increase the profits of, other classes of the community. Does the farmer want to build, say, a wire fence — he is taxed to support some petty wiredrawer that says he cannot otherwise live. Or does he want twine to bind his grain, he has to pay so much tax to feed some 'infant manufacturer.' Does he want any new implement, even if none of the kind is made in the country, he must pay one third more than it is worth — for fear some other 'infant' is not well fed, and so on through a great many other items.

In our view, 'Protection' means robbing somebody else. . . . This is unreasonable. The farmer ought not to be compelled to submit to extortion.

The farmer has to take his products abroad and sell them in the open market of the world, but he cannot purchase in that market what he wants, without paying a bounty (in the form of protective duties) collected from him before or as soon as he brings it into the country; for the benefit of the home manufacturer. In other words, he is compelled to pay, out of what he gets for his unprotected produce, a tax, to enable the protected manufacturer to make a greater profit on what he produces.

Now, what does the farmer get for this forced tribute to the manufacturer? He gets nothing.

In conclusion, we wish no exclusive privileges for any. The prosperity of agriculture, commerce and manufactures depends on the same foundation. The one cannot reap any advantage from the depression of the other.[16]

There was the additional extortion of price-fixing combines which accompanied the protectionism of the times and affected everything from salt to flour, oats to cotton, binder twine to wholesale groceries, fire insurance to transportation services. Salt is a vital ingredient in cheesemaking and was purchased by the ton by every cheese factory — much of it, in those days, from Goderich. Yet when a merchant in Huron County broke ranks and began selling salt below combine prices, a judge in Goderich ruled in favour of an injunction taken out against him.[17]

There was much to complain about in rural Ontario. Yet with the Mowat government having abandoned traditional liberalism in free trade and small business enterprise, there was no outlet for these complaints in either of the traditional political parties.[18] Many returned to the agrarian reform movement which had been dormant since the crushing of the 1837 Rebellion. Its latest manifestation was called the Patrons of Industry, founded in the United States.

Like the Reformers led by William Lyon MacKenzie in the early 1800s, the Patrons wanted an egalitarian society where wealth, power, and privilege were based on the labour of people's hands, not on capital with its greater capacity for concentration and, thus, for fostering social disparities. The farmer, they maintained, was the founding "patron" of all industry.[19] Farmers, however, and the rural economy generally, were being stifled by the exclusive monopolies associated with the railways and other combines, plus the protected manufacturers and the merchant bankers in the cities. Singling out the railway monopoly created by the merger of the Grand Trunk and the Great Western, the Patrons' newspaper, the *Farmer Sun*, argued: "Cheap railway rates are a necessity if the majority of our people are not to become mere hewers of wood and drawers of water to the bondholders of Canadian railways."[20]

Politically, the Patrons represented a challenge to the consolidation of power and capital occurring with the increasing scope and scale of industrialization. They wanted fewer privileges for the "non-labouring, non-producing classes." Accordingly, they were against monopolies and combines.[21] They also favoured currency reform and liberalization of banking, and more participatory democracy, through referenda.

To by-pass the price-fixing combine on salt, they leased a salt mine and established a cooperative for distributing salt to members. They also started the Patron Cordage and Implement Co.[22]

In 1893, the Patrons became a political party, though seeking no more than the balance of power, to leverage the Liberals back to classical small-propertied liberalism. A year later, they basically achieved their goal as they elected 17 members to the provincial legislature, including D.M. McPherson of Lancaster. Within four years, however, the Patrons were pushed into political oblivion, with no members re-elected. Partly, they'd been discredited through a smear campaign associating them with the racist Protestant Protective Association, which took seven seats in the 1894 election.[23] But they also failed in their attempts to broaden support from a romantic bond among farmers to include a workable alliance with industrial trade unions.[24] Neither the Patrons nor the United Farmers of

Top: Tavistock Union Cheese & Butter Factory established in 1878.

Bottom: East Zorra and Blandford Cheese and Butter Factory near Innerkip, Ontario, circa 1910.

Ontario, which succeeded them — with slogans like "Good Roads for All" — resolved the conflicting conceptions of people who worked with their hands, either as hired hands working for wages or as autonomous craftspersons, self-employed professionals, and yeomen.[25] One group was working class, with no control over the "means of production." The other group, owning land and controlling the tools of production at least, was considered middle class. Finally, the Patrons disappeared because, while they were clear in what they opposed, they lacked a practicable sense of how to achieve their vision of an egalitarian, small-is-beautiful political economy in a society already stamped in the mould of large-scale capital and bureaucratic systems.

The defeat of the Patrons and their successors associated with the United Farmers, who formed the government in the early 1920s, though only briefly, marks the fading of an older vision of Ontario. After that, it no longer seemed conceivable for urban and rural interests associated with locally owned, small-scale operations to unite in common purpose. And no one could imagine a continuity between modern factory workers and traditional craftspeople, including farm-based women cheesemakers. No one could imagine a basis for solidarity around the craft orientation of doing a thing as best one can, for the pride and pleasure of good creative effort, not simply for the sake of money.

Meanwhile, unionization of Britain's industrial working class had brought a measure of progress to the average working family. Meat was replacing cheese as the staple source of protein. Exports of Ontario cheddar began to drop through the 1920s. Farmers and cheesemakers were left to respond as best they could, individually. Blessed with the rich soil of Southwestern Ontario, farmers there left dairying for the more lucrative cash crops of tobacco, corn, tomatoes, and other vegetables. In the Central and Eastern regions, where thinner, poorer soils constrained alternatives but where the distance to the Montreal market was at least shorter, cheese factories remained central to the rural economy.

Still, cheddar cheese making was a way of life that had grown up with the province of Ontario. It would take a long time for the craft, and the culture that it embodied, to wither away. Meanwhile, it remained the first job off the farm for thousands of farm boys and the main source of cash income for 35 per cent of the farmers of Ontario.[26]

Poor returns drove many out. It kept others from modernizing, which left them increasingly out of step with the times. But as long as they carried on, it didn't seem to matter. Nothing seemed to change. Cheesemaking was still a small-scale craft supported by old-fashioned technology and a philosophy of getting by without electricity, without refrigeration, and without decent sanitation facilities. Cheesemakers focused on making the best cheddar cheese they could, for the exacting export market.

While the rest of the province moved forward to the quick-step beat of technological time, the cheese factories remained on traditional organic time. They opened and closed with the seasons. Cheesemakers paced their work to the time it took for milk to ripen and cheese to age, naturally. And when they told a story, they gave it the time it took for the story to tell itself.

I listened to the stories, and among them I caught a faint echo of Donald Menzies, one-time cheesemaker at Molesworth and one-time guardian to my father.

A Day at the Cheese Factory

The cheese factory was the hub of every old Ontario rural community and the centre of the local economy. As farmers waited to deliver their milk, they caught up on each other's business — whether a new bull was performing and who was seen talking to whom. They also watched the cheesemaker carefully. They waited to see what he'd do about the farmer who was adulterating his milk or taking more than his share of whey home to feed his pigs.

John Fraser of Vankleek Hill told the story of his father Neil. In 1890, at the age of 20, Neil Fraser was hired as cheesemaker at a factory across the Ottawa River at St. Joseph du Lac in Quebec. One of the bigger patrons was known for getting his way, including bringing an extra milk can along some mornings and helping himself to more than his portion of whey from the whey tank behind the factory. Fraser let him carry on for a while until he thought he knew what was what. Then one morning, he waited till the farmer had put the lids back on his milk cans, including the one that he'd brought along on his milk wagon empty. Fraser suddenly jumped onto the wagon and, taking the lid of the first can off, he dumped the whey back into the whey tank. He set the can down and slammed on the lid with a crash that reverberated through the crowd of watchful farmer-patrons. He turned to the second can, threw its lid aside and emptied that one too. Slam. And the next. The total was what Neil figured the patron had taken beyond his quota. Then he jumped off the wagon and went on with his work in the cheese factory.

He kept his rifle by his bed that night and, for the next few days, leaned it against the wall by the milk-receiving platform. But nothing happened. And at the end of the season, the farmer-patrons took him to town and outfitted him with a suit, his first.[1]

The close watching went both ways. One day at the Rosedale Cheese Factory, in Lanark County, the cheesemaker James Drew and his assistant Norm Dunlop were settling down to the day's cheesemaking when they realized the McMunn's milk hadn't come in. The family had been delivering milk every day of the week for two generations and never missed a day, so they believed something was wrong. Norm took a run down the road to the farm. He found the McMunn's cows huddled up by the closed barn door, their milk bags achingly bloated. But there was no one at home — not the McMunns nor their hired hand, Harvey McIntyre. As it turned out, Keith and Margaret McMunn had gone off visiting, leaving Harvey to do the chores. But the man had gone to town on Saturday night and gotten into a brawl. This left him in the Almonte lock-up and the McMunns' cows locked out of their milking stalls. The assistant cheesemaker and a neighbour, Mr. Vines, opened the barn door, did the milking, and took the milk back to the cheese factory.[2]

While the tall tales were being told and the last of the milk haulers were turning their horses homeward, the cheesemaker was already hard at work with his craft. Steam piped from the boiler to the cheese vats was warming the milk to the desired 86° F, and the flywheel off the generator was ready to turn. You could hear the kerflap-kerflap-kerflap of the belt carrying the power from the flywheel to the line-shaft above each vat and a muffled burring as iron gears turned the arms of the agitator and, in the better models, sent them travelling up and down the length of the oblong vat.[3] The resident cat slipped by like a shadow, seeking a place to snooze. Vapours rose from the open vats, invisible yet dense, thickly sweet with lactose laced with the surfacing tang of lactic acid.

Cheesemaking involves three processes: working up the acid with heat and bacteria, curdling, and working out the whey from the cheese curd. Developing the ferment, working up the acid, or "ripening" the cheese milk as it's also called, is the central process. It involves converting milk sugar called lactose into lactic acid, then building up the acid to just the right point, and stopping it there with cold water, then salt. The conversion is triggered by lactic-acid bacteria, which in traditional "raw-milk" cheddar was simply whatever strain was growing naturally in the milk when it was delivered to the cheese factory.

In the "heat-treated" process, the milk is initially heated to a point just short of pasteurization (145° F., or 68° C.), which kills off most resident bacteria, the good ones as well as the bad.[4] In the totally mechanized and even automated process, the milk is pasteurized, which kills all the natural bacteria, including those

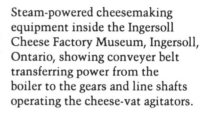

Steam-powered cheesemaking equipment inside the Ingersoll Cheese Factory Museum, Ingersoll, Ontario, showing conveyer belt transferring power from the boiler to the gears and line shafts operating the cheese-vat agitators.

crucial to proper ripening of cheese in the aging process.

To compensate for the deactivated natural bacteria, the cheesemaker adds some "starter culture," a single known strain of lactic-acid bacteria. This greatly simplifies the business of making cheese. In the case of pasteurized cheesemaking, which is the way most Ontario cheddar is made nowadays, the milk becomes inert through pasteurization. Because of this, the cheese can be made according to a fixed recipe and timetable, and the whole process can be automated. But there is a trade-off: eliminating the wild diversity of naturally occurring bacteria produces a more predictable but also decidedly less flavourful cheddar cheese. Even heat-treated cheese lacks the pungency and full-bodied flavour of raw-milk cheddar. The difference between raw-milk cheese and pasteurized cheese, even hand-made and well-aged versions of it, is akin to the difference between a superb vintage red wine and good table wine.

When Fred Day attended dairy school in the winter of 1941, he learned to let the acid level of the milk advance by .01 per cent before adding rennet to coagulate the milk into curd. But experience taught him to let it go three points: "The milk often started around .16 — the stuff in those days, look at it, and it'd go sour. I'd only put a certain amount of steam on the vats, to warm them slowly (to 86 degrees). That way the vat set quickly, if the rennet was any good."[5]

Rennet is a protein enzyme found only in the fourth stomach of a milk-fed calf. Although the early cheesemakers made their own rennet extracts from calf stomachs pledged by farmer-patrons, by the late 1800s rennet extracts — like starter cultures and cheesecloth and dye for orange cheese — were available from travelling suppliers. Rennet will coagulate a vat of milk in 20 minutes if the acid is advanced enough and the temperature is around 90° F. Coagulation serves to trap the important parts of milk — the butterfat, the calcium, and other solids — in a gel of casein, from which the water will be slowly extracted through the subsequent cooking stage, leaving an increasingly firm curd for making cheese. It is important not to cut the curd too soon, before the gel is firm enough to act like a sponge and hold the constituent elements. It is equally important not to wait too long, for the curd might become too brittle, and either the gel will shatter or the resultant curds won't release their watery whey.[6]

This is where skill and dedicated perception come into cheesemaking, the last of Ontario's hand-craft industries. Some of the cheesemakers just used their finger, sliding it into the jellied milk, watching for a clean break in the gel mass and feeling the satin near-solid against their fingers. As Fred Day put it after some 40 years making cheese, at Newark, at Zenda, at Britton Factory, then at Atwood: "You go by the feel a lot. If you didn't have any feeling in your fingertips, why you were in trouble."

For nearly a century, the curd was cut by hand, using what were officially called "curd knives" but known locally as "harps." There were two of these devices, each a series of wires stretched across a roughly square frame. In one, the wires were strung horizontally and in the other, vertically. When placed side by side, frame to frame in a cheese vat, they just fit the width of it. Then, with one on one side of the cheese vat and another holding the other opposite him, they drew the wire-frame curd knives down the length of the vat. Switching sides, they then drew the curd knives back again, thus sectioning the jelly-curd into quarter-inch cubes. They let it rest for a bit, then notched up the steam running through the jackets under the vats, put the power back on the agitator, and began to cook or cure the curd, very slowly at first so as not to break the gel. Slowly the ferment developed, and the thickened milk resolved itself into something reasonably firm.

One of Doug Rowe's first chores as a boy was helping his widowed mother run the Champion Cheese factory at Cold Spring: "They didn't have much equipment in them times. As I recall, they had a small steam engine and agitators to stir the milk. But if they happened to have a breakdown in the steam engine, why you made the cheese by hand."[7]

Developing the ferment took a couple of hours, a time when cheesemakers bandaged their cheese for storage, often using old flour bags. They also turned the cheeses in the curing room, greasing the tops and checking for skimmers, the larvae of the cheese fly. They also cut fresh cheesecloth ready for hooping that day's cheese. It was a busy time with all the things that always needed doing, but not so busy that you couldn't stop for a visit when one of the suppliers dropped by to see if you needed any cultures, or salt, or cheesecloth, or dye for orange cheese. As Fred Day recalled:

They were the old-time salesmen, and they'd go from factory to factory. They'd generally have a little basket to carry a crock with them. I don't know how much got sold, but you had a sociable time with them. This one guy, Mallard — when he died, he gave $50 to Charlie Riley, the guy that carried the basket. He said, "When I die, I'll probably be buried in Dundas; so you get a room in the hotel there and invite the guys in and buy em a drink." So up we went; there was nothing sad about it.

If the culture was good and the acid was coming up fine, the whey would be ready to run in an hour and a half. "It'd depend on how your acidity was coming," Fred Day explained. "You wouldn't do the same thing every day. If you had a poor culture, that'd give a lot of headaches."

Fred used to grab a bit of curd between his

Top Left: Testing the curd by hand in the whey bath.

Top Right: Lloyd Steacy of the Forfar Dairy piling matted curd.

Bottom: Curd racks, Millbank Cheese Factory.

thumb and forefinger. But he also used the acidimeter. At Plum Hollow, Claude Flood trusted his senses. Dipping a hand into the misty-yellow soup of curds and whey, he'd bring out a good handful of curd:

You can pretty near tell by the feel of the curd when it's ready to run. When it's ready to run the whey off. So you just reach in and grab a handful of curd as the agitator's going through, and you give that a feel there. You squeeze it up tight, and then you just open up your hand, and it just springs right out. That's if it's comin' pretty good. If it's workin' good. A week ago, we got some penicillin in. That's death to cheese.

Penicillin can enter the process through milk from a cow being treated for an illness or infection; it kills the bacteria, producing a "slow" or "dead" vat.

After the whey was drained off — or dipped off into a curd sink as they did in Western Ontario — the real work began. This was stirring the curd which, in the early days was done entirely by hand, supplemented by a curd rake, also worked by hand. Gordon Henry, the former Mayor of Ingersoll, told me his first job was working in a cheese factory, and it was nothing but hard manual work. "I wore my fingers right up to my elbow stirring curd," he said. He knew he was moving up in the world when, in 1934, he took a job with Canada Packers heaving sides of beef and pork around for 35 cents an hour.[8]

Working the curd was a tricky business, a balancing act between keeping the whey draining and letting the curds rest so they could mat for the cheddaring stage. The timing was important too, since acid development would continue until the curds were milled and salted. Too much acid development, often coupled with too much heat in the cooking and stirring phase, produced a sour-tasting cheese with a crumbly, mealy texture. But if you didn't get all the moisture out, the cheese was pasty soft and had a smell like day-old tinned pineapple.[9]

With the whey pretty well drained away, cheesemakers shovelled the curd granules into piles along the length of the vat and let them mat together. Once it was a solid mass, they took a long-bladed knife and cut it into rectangular chunks and layers. They laid these on top of each other, turning and cutting them again every 15 minutes or so, and relayering them until the matted curd looked and felt ready for the final step of milling and salting.

Claude Flood knew it was ready when the slabs of curd looked "slicky." To Glen Martin at the Pine River Cheese factory, it looked "like beefsteak."[10] Harold Kingston, cheesemaker at Napanee and later at Harrowsmith, described this process differently:

Talmage Stone (above) *inside the storage room of the Forfar Cheese Factory* (below).

The old fella I learned from, he'd take his finger and just dig in and pull it up, and if it pulls up like a chicken breast — like if you take and tear the meat off a chicken breast, why, you know how it'll come up stringy? Well, when your cheese'll do that, you're not far off. Because if it's acidy there, it'll break. And if it hasn't got enough acid, why it's gonna be soft; too rubbery. And I say there's some people can spend all their lives making cheese and never be a cheesemaker. You have to have a feel, a sense of feel, I guess. You can tell when the curd's cooked. It's springy. If it stays in a ball, it's not cooked. And then if the curd wasn't cooked enough, why you stir it more, get it drier. That'll help out your cook a little. Then when you salt, why you put on more salt; that'll flush out more whey.[11]

And so it went, one organic process helping or offsetting another, each at its own particular pace. When the curd had been milled into four-to five-inch strips, it was stirred for half an hour or so, until the curds were smooth and silky.

Then it was salted, at a rate of two to three pounds of salt per 1,000 pounds of milk, and the salt was thoroughly mixed in.[12] Finally the curd was shovelled and funnelled into cheese hoops, lined with cheesecloth drawn over a metal bandager, which was pulled out of the hoop once the cheesecloth bandage had been filled with curd inside. With a cheesecloth cap on top, plus the metal folla or follower, the cheese was ready for pressing in the gang press, where pressure is exerted through a series of interlocking gears and a lever at one end.

In the early days, when cheese was made twice daily, except on Sunday, a cheesemaker was lucky to be out of the factory by eight or nine at night. Fred Day nearly quit after his first day making cheese at a factory on his own. This was at Newark. He didn't know whether it was the milk or the culture that was slow, or whether the rennet was off or he was. He didn't leave the factory until 11 o'clock that night. "If this is cheesemaking," he told himself, "I don't think I'm gonna stay at it." But farm labouring, where he'd started, appealed to him even less. He stayed and became one of the best among a select group of generally anonymous men who were considered the finest cheesemakers in the world. In 1948, he won the Champion and Grand Champion Awards for the highest-scoring cheddar at the Royal Winter Fair, and in 1949, he came second at the British Empire Show in Belleville. His wife Edith kept track of these triumphs in the family scrapbook and photo album.

Claude Flood's Culture

Years after Claude Flood had passed away and the Plum Hollow Cheese Factory was forced to close, Jack Beaton, a supplier with Miles Laboratories and long-time director of the Western Ontario Dairymen's Association, still remembered the Claude Flood culture.

"It was as contrary as the people of Leeds County. You couldn't kill it with a stick."[1]

Claude Flood was famous for the culture he used in his cheesemaking. So famous that cheesemakers came from great distances to get what they called a "pup" of the stuff. Dairy Branch scientists at the Kemptville Dairy School, and even at Guelph, called it "the Claude Flood starter," as though it were a patented and commercial strain of bacteria.[2]

Claude Flood never charged for it, nor did he know the science of what he was doing. But he did know his craft, and he practised it rigorously and with an abiding personal commitment. This included making up a fresh batch of starter culture every day and taking the trouble to get it right every time. One of the things people always remembered about the quiet-spoken little cheesemaker from Plum Hollow was that "he was always washing his hands," and his factory was equally clean.[3]

"The first thing about a cheese factory is to

keep it clean," he told me. The second was: "We had a system for everything."

He started the culture-making process during the first lull of the day, as the milk was ripening in the cheese vats prior to setting with rennet. Leaving his wife Ella and, later, his assistant, Lewis, watching the vats in the factory, he carried a quart-sealer jar full of the morning's milk over to the house, along with the jar of yesterday's starter. He placed this in the slow-cooker well at the back of the stove and, after first heat-treating it, got out the silver baby spoon which he used for "innoculating" the culture by adding just a little of the leftover culture from yesterday to the still-warm milk. Then, putting the lid on the slow cooker and setting the heat at low, he left the new culture to grow there in the kitchen. It is important that he did this work in the house, well away from the bacteriophage virus which lurked everywhere there was whey in and around the factory itself. Also, he scrubbed his hands thoroughly after coming up from the factory to the house, though whether he knew much about bacteria is far from certain.

Claude Flood grew up in Eastern Ontario near what was dubbed the "cradle of Canadian Orangeism," Brockville.[4] He attended the local separate school where teachers' salaries were about half the rate for local public-school teachers, which in turn were about half the rate for teachers in the towns and cities.[5] "One teacher," Claude recalled, "maybe she went to high school for one year; she was nice enough all right, but I don't think she put too much information into your head. The next girl, she didn't have too much education either." He left after grade six, and soon was working as a cheesemaker's assistant, which generally means a lot of scrubbing of vats and curd sinks and curd mills and so on for very little money. But he learned the virtue of silent perseverance and eventually became a maker. When he started working as the cheesemaker at Plum Hollow, one of the patrons took offence and came to see the owner, John Tackaberry.

"I see you have yourself a new cheesemaker."

"Yep."

"I hear he's a Catholic."

"Yep, and a damn good one."

The patron took his milk elsewhere, but Tackaberry stuck by a good and dependable cheesemaker. Over the years, Claude came to own that plant, producing prize-winning cheese year after conscientious year.

As an old man, widowed and living a parsimonious existence in the old frame house beside the factory, he talked about his work, while carefully folding the uneaten half of a muffin into a cellophane wrapper. His skin was transparent over a ruddy, gaunt face. Big ears stuck out on either side. He looked up:

If I had my life to live over again, I guess I'd want to use it still making cheese. I suppose I'm bragging, but I usually made good cheese. Of course, I never had 100 per cent; one year, I had four boxes (out of 6,000) of second-grade cheese. That was just one small vat.

I didn't want to be at the bottom. I always tried to get better. I put in a lot of hours and I went along as best I could.

Tears blurred the surface of his clear blue eyes. The old man rose, put the muffin away in the bread box, and returned to the table with a rag for the crumbs. His big, bony hands were red and knuckled from a lifetime's dedication to his craft, working from five in the morning till nine at night, and even later if he was out on farm visitations.

Claude Flood, Cheesemaker, Plum Hollow.

Sanitation and Cheese Factory Inspectors

Certain themes ran like arteries through the stories old cheesemakers told me. One of these was the vital importance of cleanliness.

It was Jack Bain's most vivid memory from his apprenticeship with cheesemaker W.C. Laughlin at a little cheese factory near London starting in 1918:

My first job was grubbin' along after him. I recall that he wanted everything clean. I'd work Saturday nights in them days; the older boys would be wantin' to go to town. I'd be 15.

The wooden slats of the curd sinks, they were the devil to clean. You had to get down in there with a brush and really clean that out. That was the main part of the cheese business in them days, was to keep things clean; because you didn't have the sterilizers and one thing and another.[1]

In the early days, the cheesemakers and their associations were entirely responsible for keeping up standards. Gradually, however, the provincial government became involved, emphasizing the science of cheesemaking and the science of "sanitation." By 1906, the Agriculture Department had 30 cheese instructor-inspectors across the province, including two sanitation inspectors.[2]

Until about the 1930s, the focus was on instruction. Inspectors helped cheesemakers operate the Babcock butterfat tester to police adulteration. When regulations for sediment testing were introduced in 1914, they helped them do tests for that. Then, with the introduction of regulations in 1926 requiring tests for fermentation, they gave instructions on how to perform the Methylene Blue Reduction Fermentation Test to detect sour milk coming in from the farm.

It is not known how many cheesemakers actually did all these tests, or had the necessary "dairy plant environment equipped with minimum laboratory capability," in the words of one of the long-time inspection administrators with the Dairy Branch.[3]

Most cheesemakers had only a grade-eight education, if that.[4] They'd also learned cheesemaking as a craft, not a science, through a two- or three-year apprenticeship. Many didn't have a dairy school diploma which had been an official requirement since 1909 for anyone operating a cheese factory in Ontario. The diploma conferred on the cheesemaker the province's authority to grade and test farmers' milk and to uphold proper sanitation procedures in the factory and on farm dairies. In 1926, the Dairy Products Act moved to enforce this regulation, first conferring certificates on cheesemakers with three years' experience running a cheese factory who didn't have a dairy school diploma.[5]

Transportation was another barrier. The best instruction was concentrated in Western Ontario. In 1914, the Dairymen's Association of Eastern Ontario lobbied the Agriculture Department to increase staff at the Eastern Dairy School in Kingston and to do "more efficient" research.[6]

Many factories weren't properly licensed either, although this had been a requirement since 1909. Nor did they have the kind of equipment that was expected. Farmers on the board of directors objected to wasting money on Babcock butterfat testers. Even where equipment was available, many loudly doubted the results and the cheesemaker's competence in producing them.[7]

The milk-adulteration problem, at least, was finally settled in 1920, when the newly elected United Farmers of Ontario (UFO) passed long-overdue legislation making the Babcock test mandatory and linking farmers' milk payments directly to the test results. In 1926, the government appointed the first four of what would soon be a full staff of check testers to ensure enforcement across the province's 1,000 cheese and butter plants.

As for the other tests, it's possible that many cheesemakers relied on the somewhat simpler techniques associated with the senses. They looked inside a farmers' milk cans after emptying them at the milk-receiving stand. If there was dirt in the bottom, that was evidence no patron could dispute. Similarly, a quick sniff when he took off the lid of the milk can was still a reliable indication of milk quality.

There are no recorded cases of food poisoning from Ontario cheddar cheese reports Dr. Arthur Hill, Assistant Professor of Food Science at the University of Guelph. No disasters happened. But gradually, the makers of Ontario cheddar were seen as having fallen behind prevailing standards simply because they didn't seem to have many formal and enforceable ones. As well, many of the new standards were established in the cities. The ones concerning hygiene and sanitation were particularly relevant there, where concentrated populations made it vital to check diseases such as diphtheria and tuberculosis which were spread through water and milk. In 1906, the Ottawa Dairy began pasteurizing and bottling milk for drinking.[8] Soon, municipal boards of health, often under pressure by public-health-conscious women's groups, began requiring that local drinking milk be pasteurized.

Jack Bain,
Cheesemaker, Cheesemaking Instructor, Cheese Factory Inspector.

James L. Baker,
Dairy Commissioner.

Former Dairy Commissioner Jim Baker felt the cheese factories were allowed to get away with low standards. "We had some pretty gosh-awful factories. But only a few, really, and mostly in Eastern Ontario," he added.[9] In Eastern Ontario, money had always been tight, and instruction had been rather thin.

Jack Bain, who succeeded Frank Herns as head cheese instructor for Western Ontario in 1942, had a more sympathetic view of cheese-makers' and farmers' hygienic practices. It was also an insider's perspective, for he had worked as a cheesemaker for 24 years and had grown up on what he called "a one-horse farm" in Oxford County:

Most of the farmers knew about sanita-tion. Oh, some of them slipped, y'know. It took a lot of water to keep things clean, and some of them didn't use quite enough. You didn't have a whole lot of water in them days, y'know, just a couple of tea kettles on the stove and that's what you had to wash four big cans with, and they did the best they could.

Jack Bain was one of the last of the old breed of instructor-inspectors. He came up through the ranks. He not only made cheese, and showed it in London, Toronto, and at the British Empire Championships in Belleville, where he won the top prizes several years in a row. He was also active in the county cheesemakers' association and the Dairymen's Association of Western Ontario. And he continued the tradition of sup-plementing the associations' guild-like efforts at self-help and self-policing:

We did a lot of work in the industry through our associations. But we had to get through some legislation so we could go talk to the fella. Quite a few farmers had to be taken to court for adulteration. They thought it was all right to throw in a little water. Some of them wouldn't believe the fat test when it come up. They wouldn't believe anybody could tell how much fat there was in a hundredweight of milk. But after a couple of years it was accepted.

The cheesemakers were usually happy to see you. You'd go in and spend two or three days. And if they wanted to make exhibition cheese, why you'd help them select the milk and we'd run tests on the milk and give them an idea of where to look for trouble. And if there was anything new — any cultures or anything, why we had the information and we'd talk to them.

Bain acted as a go-between on problems arising in the industry, alerting the researchers at the Ontario Agricultural College when there was a problem that needed investigating and passing on the results of their latest research, published in their bulletins. "And the different wrappers"

— plastic and waxed paper, tinfoil and plastic — "oh, what we went through on them. I worked with the people who made the wraps, and we'd take a half a dozen out and have the cheesemakers try them out in different factories." Sitting forward, big hands outstretched on his knees in a modest apartment in London, Ontario, the retired head of the cheese division for the Ontario Dairy Branch laughed at the things he and his staff got up to:

I've examined cheese on the steps of the parliament buildings and in cars at night . . . And with waxed cheese. Oh, the Englishmen wouldn't take it. "It wouldn't age right," they said. But I made waxed cheese ever since I started, and I sold 'em.

You got to know your men and how to get your point across. Some, you could come straight to the point. Others, why, you'd build up slowly. And then, why, we all spoke the same language.

"Missionary Work"

At cheesemakers' meetings, they called it their "missionary work" or their "farm visitations." This was the delicate and sometimes difficult business of dealing with farmers whose milk was a little off or too thinned down with water. It didn't matter that a law passed in 1909 gave cheesemakers the authority to reject a farmer's milk at the cheese factory. Nor that another law, passed in 1927, authorized cheesemakers to enter farm premises on the trail of milk which was producing gassy, second-grade cheese.[1]

Each community was its own little world, with its own power bases and its own sense of justice. The cheesemaker had to work his way carefully, to maintain his standards as best he could, while also keeping his job at the local factory.

Meek, slight-of-build Russ Martin hadn't been cheesemaker at the Molesworth Cheese and Butter Factory very long before he nearly lost his job for rejecting a patron's milk as sour. Worse, he couldn't get in touch with the farmer to forewarn him and perhaps give him an alternative to having his milk sent publicly home with the milk drawer:

They just had a little one-horse phone company there at Molesworth, and I couldn't phone out, so I couldn't get through. So anyway, he was mad as heck. He was going to call a meeting and have me put out. So anyway, he come up here, and I told him I couldn't leave the place here because the milk was comin' in and all. Well, he didn't believe me. He was goin' to call

Harold Kingston, Cheesemaker, Morden and Harrowsmith Cheese Factories.

Russ Martin, Cheesemaker, Molesworth Cheese Factory.

that meetin' and have me fired. Anyway, then he found out. The problem was the little gasoline engine he used to cool the milk had conked out on him; the gas tank leaked. Anyway, he was man enough to come back and apologize; y'see, he wasn't accustomed to having milk sent home; he took a lot of pride in it.[2]

It wasn't much easier where cheesemakers owned their own factories. Disgruntled patrons could simply take their milk elsewhere. No matter what, cheesemakers had to walk a fine line, being tough enough to keep up standards yet diplomatic enough to keep up the business.

If it was something simple like dirty milk cans, Russ Martin sent a little note home with the cans, discreetly tucked inside for none but the farmer to see and read. "And if there was some odour on the milk or something, why maybe you'd go out and try to figure out what was wrong. I'd just tell them, 'milk wasn't too good this morning, and wondered what was wrong.' Oh, it was usually pretty easy; either the milk wasn't cooled well or the cows got into the turnips and ate the turnip tops." Turnip tops and leeks, which grew wild in many of the wooded areas where farmers pastured their cows, left an odour on the milk that got into the cheese.

In Hastings County, Central Ontario, Harold Kingston regularly made up little jam-jar lots of cheese from individual patrons' milk to trace the source of trouble in the cheese vat. It was something he started when working for farmer cooperatives and continued after he bought his own factory at Harrowsmith and officially became his own boss. It was a lot of work, adding a bit of rennet to each jar, cutting the curd with his pocketknife. But it was worth the effort, as he explains:

Farmers, a lot of them, are a hard lot to deal with, and when you went out, you had to know what you were talkin' about. And that was one way, in my way of thinkin', that I could prove what I was talkin' about. I had them sayin', "There's nothin' wrong with my milk." And I'd just say, "Well, you better straighten it up, or I'm gonna send it home."

One lad, he took a pitchfork, and he was gonna put me right out of the barn. He looked at the sample and he just said, "Well, that's not my milk." And I just said, "Well, it is," and he just grabbed the pitchfork and he said, "You get out of here, and don't you ever come back." And I said: "That's fine. But," I said, "until you straighten up that milk, it's not comin' in that plant."

You won't find too many cheesemakers who back up too much. You just couldn't.

Once, when he was still working for the farmer cooperative at Morden, Harold rejected milk from the president of the cooperative himself. Word spread quickly, and by afternoon his wife Hazel heard the story at a Women's Institute meeting. Another time, Harold recalled, "this one fella in particular, I sent his milk home three days, morning, night and everything. Three days, till he cleaned it up. And he cleaned it up, but he never admitted to me he did." But on one of those days, Harold dropped by the local garage. As Harold tells the story:

The owner said, "I had one of your patrons in here today." And I said, "Oh, dirty milkin' machine?" It was so clogged with rotten, congealed milk the farmer couldn't get it open himself. And he said "Yeah." And I said, "Well, who is it?" And he said, "well, I'm not gonna tell who." And I said, "well, I'll tell you who it is." So I told him, and he kind of laughed.

At Plum Hollow, Claude Flood was somewhat milder in his approach:

I remember once a farmer's wife told me, "We always have trouble in the summer. There's some kind of weed grows in the swamp where our cows are, and they eat that, and it leaves this green slime [inside the milking machine]." So I showed her a couple of times just what to do and, well, I guess the weed quit growin'.

The slightest of smiles. A quick look in the eye to see whether I'd got it. The old man went on:

I always had good visits. But you always had five or maybe six that were just careless. There was one fella, just a young fella; he wasn't married yet. And one day when he was in, I said, "Don, I think you're takin' your cans over to the tank where the calves are drinking out of, and washing them out in that. That's what it smells to me like you're doin'." Anyway, he went over to the general store over there, and he said, "That Flood, he can just look at your cans, and tell you what you've done wrong." So I guess I hit the nail. But he got better.

And then some people were a bit short, and you had to hit them at just the right time. There was this one hired man, and the wife didn't want to tell him because she was afraid of losing him, and her husband was away a lot working on the highway. So I waited a little while, and then one day, I felt it was just about right to tell him, because he was a bit short. He didn't like to be told.

Adulteration was the worst problem, especially during the years before butterfat testing was made compulsory; then the instructor-inspectors could be called on to deal with it. That left only the occasional problem of skimming off a little cream.

"I've been to places for an evening, and they'd serve cake and whipped cream or something like this. But I never said anything," Russ Martin told me. "Oh, I didn't blame them. They weren't really cheating, and they didn't all do it. And if they cheated too much, why they'd lose out on their test." From the time the Babcock tester was introduced until its use was enforced by legislation, more and more factories voted to have their cheese proceeds based on their individual scores on the butterfat test as the best way to guard against adulteration.

The evening visits helped maintain good relations between the cheesemaker and the patrons. Each needed the other and, for as long as the cheese factory was the axis of the local community, the proceeds from steady sales of Grade A cheese kept them united in a common cause.

Cheese Boards and Market Control

Jack Bain shook his head. "The cheese industry was always in trouble," he told me with a rueful, weathered smile. At the heart of all those troubles — if not creating them, then aggravating them, prolonging them, and eventually rendering them incurable — was money. Lack of money. Many cheese factories were built on a mortgage, and many closed for failing to meet the payments. The cheese market, like any world market, especially for perishable commodities, was chronically lurching from bust to bust. It looked up only occasionally in between.

This wasn't entirely the result of natural market forces, however. It was the result of powerful vested interests dating back to the earliest days of British mercantile imperialism. Very simply, British cheese merchants controlled the cheese market from the earliest days of Ontario cheddar. They set the terms of trade. They set the price that farmers would get for their cheddar at something only fractionally above the lowest cost of production. Nothing was done to offset this power locally, and little was done to mitigate dependency on the British importers.

If anything, the cheese boards reinforced the powerlessness and dependency by masking them under a patina of competitive bidding. The first cheese-marketing board, or simply "cheese board" as it was commonly named, was opened in Ingersoll in 1873, with others organized a little later in Stratford and Belleville.[1] By 1920, there were 14 cheese boards in Central and Eastern Ontario, including one at Oxford Station operated by Jim Sanderson, who opened the first refrigerated cheese storage business in Eastern Ontario in 1930.[2] Another at Vankleek Hill was associated with Neil Fraser, who by then had diversified into cheese supplies, transport, and warehousing. By this time the largest boards, such as the one at Belleville, had their own premises.

The board's cheese markets were often weekly affairs, drawing in a range of buying agents representing British importers and merchants. As more than one cheesemaker observed, the buyers "constituted an important element in the life and business of the community. They were good dressers and drove good carriages"[3] with "spirited driving horses."[4] Some of the carriages were even equipped with beds for maximum flexibility during the prime cheese-buying season in the fall.[5]

The running of the "board" was a fairly simple affair. Local factories chalked up the number of cheeses they were offering for sale, using a plain chalkboard on the premises. The buyers would bid on different lots of cheese offered by the different factories by "calling" out a price they were willing to pay.[6]

The trouble was, the bidding wasn't confined to the board event. Many buyers did most of their buying through "curb sales." They approached the salesman for a certain factory on the street before or after the official "board" sale and offered to buy that factory's cheese for a fraction more than what was bid on the board. Once the practice set in, the competitive bidding on the board degenerated into a pro-forma affair. The bids were kept low by the tacit understanding among cheese buyers that the price set through whatever price the first of them "called" out when the board began would be the base price they'd have to meet or exceed in their private off-board dealings. Complicating this and further weakening the cheese patrons' position, one man sometimes served as both factory salesman and buyer for the English importing firms. Finally, cheese importers controlled the grading of cheese and used the half-cent to two-cent differential between cheese grades to their advantage. They often graded cheese No. 1 when buying it in Canada, then revised the grade downward when they placed it in the English market. As explained by one observer, "It was contended that the grades set depended more on general market conditions than on the actual quality of the article, and that there was no guarantee that the factories making the best cheese would obtain the highest price or that an improvement in quality would be recognized or rewarded."[7]

At least the grading problem was solved when the United Farmers of Ontario formed the government in 1919. They moved to end the grading scam by introducing government grading and, in cooperation with the federal government, it was made compulsory in 1923.[8]

This left the larger problem of the board system of marketing. When University of Toronto Professor W.M. Drummond wrote about the problems facing the cheese business in the 1930s, he zeroed in on the cooperative cheese boards and described them as "more or less of a farce."[9] Ten years later, agricultural historian Robert Jones simply excused the situation as

inevitable: "The British system was so well integrated that the Ontario producers found that the appointing of an agent of their own to dispose of their cheese would fail to avail them anything, and would certainly antagonize these [British] vested interests."[10]

The pattern of local marketing initiative, which could have developed out of the hopeful starts in the 1860s, had petered out by the early 1900s. The Ingersoll Cheese Company was taken over by a British firm. Thomas Ballantyne's son went to work for the British multinational Lovell and Christmas. Alex MacLaren sold out to an American company. D.M. MacPherson went bankrupt.

The collective marketing idea, pushed aside at the formation of the Dairymen's Association, resurfaced with the United Farmers of Ontario, which began buying up creameries in the 1920s.[11] They also formed their own cheese marketing board, called the United Dairymen's Cooperative, with headquarters in Montreal, the commercial capital of Canada and the centre for produce exports. Copying the example of the Quebec Cooperative Society of Cheesemakers, they set up their own cheese auction to sell cheese from farmer-owned cooperatives across Ontario. The cooperative might have been more successful if it had worked in solidarity with the farmer cooperatives in Quebec. There was yet another critical weakness, however: it wasn't compulsory that all cheese be marketed on the board. While the cooperative did provide some competition — enough, at least to incur fierce opposition from exporters — and while it did market a lot of cheese from farmer-owned factories, it never controlled more than about 15 per cent of the cheese trade.[12] It didn't have critical mass for effective marketing power.

Attempting to change this, the United Farmers government introduced legislation establishing a marketing board that would sell all patron-factory cheese and, at the end of the year, distribute the pooled proceeds to patron-farmers. Since it was a delicate matter, touching on farmers' faith in themselves and their fear of "antagonizing" the powers that be, the government agreed to subject this to a farmer referendum. The project failed to gain a majority of farmers' support before a Tory filibuster piqued Ontario's idealistic "Farmer Premier" Charles Drury into dissolving the legislature, and the United Farmers of Ontario disappeared into political oblivion in the election of 1923.[13]

The initiative was renewed in the mid-1930s when the Natural Products Marketing Act empowered a new wave of cooperatives to market farm produce and manufactures. In 1935, the Ontario Cheese Patrons (or Producers) Marketing Board was established, with headquarters in Belleville.[14] By the early part of this century, Belleville had replaced Ingersoll as the centre of Ontario's cheese industry. Farmers in Southwestern Ontario sent their milk into the more lucrative fluid trade or diversified into cash crops such as tobacco.[15]

The board was run from the grass roots up. Farmers who became presidents of their local cheese factories sat on the board of the local county cheese producers' association. If they became president of that, they attended the meetings of the larger provincial body, possibly then being elected to the board of directors and, finally, the presidency of the Cheese Producers' Marketing Board. Some of these farmers were enlightened and well-informed, with high school and even some college education. Others had simply worked their way up through local politics and personal wheeling and dealing.

Hector Arnold, from a small rocky farm in East-Central Ontario, was of the second kind. Hector Arnold was 14 when his father died, and he dropped out of school to take over the 60-acre family farm with its herd of 12 cows.[16] He was president of the Northumberland County cheese producers' association for 40 years, a member of the provincial marketing board for 23 years, and president for 10.

The cheese producers' marketing board began marketing cheese in England directly, with the president and other board members making personal trips to visit the London merchants. The board also tried to promote a domestic market for Ontario cheddar. It established its own, producer-owned cheese assembling and storage facilities. And it lobbied to require that

Dutch Clock at the Belleville Cheese Auction.

Borden Company Limited, Norwich, Ontario, circa 1913.

all Ontario cheddar be marketed through its marketing board. This was essential for the farmer-run association to muster enough control to break or even budge the long, historical pattern of low cheese prices, which by then had made cheese the poor country cousin of the modern dairy business. The cheese producers, however, were ill-equipped to take on the entrenched English importers single-handed, and by and large they failed. A 1947 government study noted that "there has been very little actual control by the cheese producers of methods of marketing overseas."[17]

Nor did their assembling and storage facilities do much to offset the long tradition of middlemen who supplied refrigerated storage, transportation, and other services, charging as much as they could get away with for doing so.[18] However, its often ill-informed efforts to change the status quo made it a moving target in the years ahead and its last president, Hector Arnold, the subject of personal vilification.

By the late 1920s, butter prices were nearly double the returns for cheese — the reverse of what they were in the early days of dairying.[19] Butter production also exceeded cheese production and had done so since 1922.[20] Partly, this was because hauling costs over still-crude rural roads were lower and many creameries, being newer and somewhat larger and more modern, were also operating year-round.

In the 1930s, many cheese factories closed, particularly in Western Ontario, as farmers switched their milk to condensed milk and milk-powder plants, which offered up to 50 cents a hundredweight more for farmers' milk.[21] Or, if they were close enough, they sold their milk to the expanding urban market for fluid, drinking milk, which was the most lucrative of all. The companies they turned to were often American branch plants. By 1939, Borden's had seven condensed milk and milk-powder plants in Ontario,[22] and a further five dairies handling fluid milk.[23]

Carnation was also branching into Canada at this time. Like Borden's, its factories tended to be large, employing 50 to 100 people. They also operated year-round, while the uninsulated, unrefrigerated cheese factories limped along with their one or two workers, closing in the late fall and reopening in April or May — that is, "if there was enough money in the kitty to fire up the boiler," as retired Dairy Commissioner Jim Baker commented wryly.[24]

Ontario cheddar struggled to survive in a shrinking English market increasingly dominated by cheaper pasteurized cheddar from New Zealand.[25] Every year it lost ground. It had already become the "balance wheel" of the dairy industry, the market into which farmers could conveniently dump their extra milk when other markets were saturated. Cheese would keep, at least better than butter and fluid milk. If this drove down cheddar prices still more, what did it matter? By the 1930s, the industry had been abused so long this way and

had declined to such a poor and impoverished state that it was becoming an embarrassment. Its low returns dragged down prices in other milk markets, and farmers wanted more. When the British market disappeared after the Second World War, Ontario cheddar, with its quaint, old-fashioned marketing plans, was seen as an annoying anachronism best got rid of.

At their meetings, the Dairymen's Association of Western Ontario talked of reviving the cheese mammoth promotions. But the marketing appeal of cheddar had shifted over the years from its taste and keeping power as a food staple to its convenience for the housewife and its packaged prettiness in party displays. The medium for the message had changed as well. It was no longer travelling extravaganza road shows but advertising delivered straight to consumers' homes through the media. James Kraft had supplied the armed forces with tins of pasteurized process cheese during World War I. After the war, he repackaged the product as a convenient five-pound loaf, under the label of Kraft cheese. He launched this new "brand-name" product in 1920 and began selling it, through ads in newspapers and magazines, across the United States and Canada.[26]

Meanwhile, reports from government inspectors lamented that "the best and the brightest young men" were not going into cheesemaking. With pay averaging little more than $1,000 a year, who could blame them?[27]

Money and the Board of Directors

Money. Everything came back to money. Many cheese factories were driven into the ground for the lack of necessary repairs and renovations. They couldn't convince the board of directors to spend the money. These were farmers who took stubborn pride in making do without modern conveniences. They couldn't see the point, or refused to. Sometimes it took more than diplomacy to convince them otherwise.

In Hastings County, Harold Kingston learned to establish his ground early. When a new man was elected president of the Morden Cheese Factory where he was engaged as cheesemaker, Harold listened agreeably as the farmer told him that he must clear any expenditure, large or small, through him first:

"Well that's just fine," I said. "But you better stick pretty close to your phone just in case something breaks down," I said. "Because I'll be phoning you to get someone to come down and fix it. Because," I said, "there's times when we can't afford to be broke down for more than 10 or 15 minutes or it'll ruin a vat."

So he kind of backed down. "We'll just leave it the way it is."

When cheesemakers met monthly at their county cheesemakers' association meetings, strategy for handling boards of directors was a frequent topic of discussion. In Western Ontario, it was Wes Krotz at Millbank who the younger cheesemakers looked up to. As Fred Day up the road in Atwood put it, "He had his foot down on the ground a little firmer, maybe, and his plant went ahead." Legend has it that this ramrod-thin man with the no-nonsense brushcut who'd started making cheese at age 12 turned the tables on the farmers who ran the venerable Millbank cheese factory. After a single year working as their cheesemaker, at the annual meeting considering whether to renew his contract, Krotz seized the initiative. He gave them three choices: fire him, sell him the plant, or give him free rein to run the factory as he saw fit. The farmers took the third choice, and the Millbank cheese factory stayed in business long after most of its neighbours had been closed and abandoned. It also had steel vats and electric agitators and lights long before Fred Day talked his board of conservative, cautious farmers at Atwood into letting him replace even the old tin-lined wooden vats that leaked like sieves from years of wear and washing:

Top Left: Millbank
Cheese and Butter Factory,
Millbank, Ontario, 1920.

Top Right: Harold Kingston and
crew repairing the curd mill.

Bottom: Wes Krotz (front and
centre), Cheesemaker, Millbank.

We used to spend all kinds of time looking for those leaks. Going over the vat with a pin, finding the holes. And then you'd have to solder them. This used to get kind of provoking. And then we had to wash under the vat, and that would stink to high heaven.

Well, I got so sick of soldering one day I told them we had to have a new vat. I think they all realized it but they hated to commit themselves.

Having finally won his point, and learned a bit in the process, Fred could pass on advice to other cheesemakers, like the shy and soft-spoken Russ Martin at Molesworth:

You don't put too much pressure on in the first meeting. You just try to get it implanted in their minds what's coming. And the next meeting, why you keep that in front of them again. And then maybe you start to put on the pressure; now, that depends on how soon you feel you have to have it. But you'd start 'em slow, you wouldn't hit 'em all at once. Now, with that vat and agitator, I worked on that one for a while. And there was some surprise too, when I mentioned the price: $1,600. But you'd keep it in front of them all the time. Maybe some of them would see that they should make this improvement. But on the other hand, they'd feel that if there was *any* possibility that I can get along without it, why they'd try to talk me down.

Fred told them that his assistant was thinking of going to another plant where more up-to-date equipment took much of the labour and clean-up out of cheesemaking; even then, one of the directors kept at him — "was it absolutely 100 per cent necessary to buy these new vats right at this moment?"

The cheese factories weren't run on the principles associated with capitalized industrial investment. There, depreciation and capital reserves are major considerations, calculated and maintained on the assumption of constant technological change and expansion. In Ontario's craft-scale cheese factories, however, the farmer-patrons didn't depreciate things, or put money aside for new and improved machines. They ran the factories the way they ran their farms, where up until the 1930s and 1940s machinery was often still secondary to their own, unpaid, manual labour. Making do, not spending money if you could possibly avoid it, was part of the rural culture. It was so far removed from its roots in mercantile banking policies and high mortgage rates that nobody really questioned it. It was in the blood of the rural-born, and Russ Martin couldn't resist its logic:

If anything broke, why it was up to me to fix it, y'see? Sometimes part of the agitator would break, and it would need soldering, and that sometimes went on into the night. . . . You always tried to save the company money, to keep it running, y'know? That's just the way I was raised. If I could fix it, why I enjoyed doing it, and it was the convenience. You generally had some old angle iron around the back there.

The biggest job he took on was when the whole grate of the old wood-coal furnace collapsed:

So that meant I had to get all the grates out and then build another bracket in there. I had to put in new bolts into the fire wall. And of course you were working inside the fire box; you had to crawl in there through the door where they shovel in the coal. But I had some old iron around that I was able to work with, and I managed to have a few big bolts around. That took most of the night, getting that done.

Russ did his own pipe fitting and soldering. "There'd be leaky valves and leaking pipes, so you'd have to fix them. Of course that would be a night job too, after the pipes had cooled down." As for learning how,

Oh, you just get into it one way or another. You'd start off on something small. Same thing with soldering. Why, I'd have farmers bringin' in their milk cans and milk pails. That's one thing I didn't like to do, because the seams on the cans would be open and the milk would get in there and sour, and you'd almost have to burn all the old solder

out to do a job, to get the solder to stick, y'see? And sometimes they'd even bring in their washing machines for me to fix, or even call me to go to their homes.

So it went, from one repair job to the next. The board of directors never put out the money to update the basic cheesemaking equipment at Molesworth, which is one of the reasons the small factory eventually had to close. Russ Martin gave it up in 1963, taking a job with Jack Bain as one of his instructor-inspectors. When he did, the more than 50 farm-families that had been Russ Martin's patrons over the years turned out in one of the worst February blizzards on record to honour the faithful cheese-maker and his wife at a supper in the Moles-worth community hall. They presented him with a small, silver-plated commemorative tray and a painting of the Molesworth Cheese Factory done by a local artist.

Not all cheesemakers worked things out or made their peace with the naysayers. At Ivanhoe in Hastings County, cheesemaker George Wood grew bitter after years of being blocked by his board of directors:

There was one fella — I won't say who — he'd never vote in favour of any new thing. He'd say, "Well, surely we don't need to buy it this year." And this would go on over and over and over. He'd never buy anything. But if you wanted to borrow a thousand dollars from him, sure he'd lend it to you.

It got to the point where Ivanhoe couldn't afford the price of wholesale modernization, and couldn't go on without it. George had seen it all along. "If you're not going ahead, you're going backwards." Eventually, the farmers sold the factory to Harold Kingston's son Bruce, who runs it still.

At dairymen's annual meetings, there were isolated stories of a new, large cheese factory being built. But most remained small, valued at little over $4,000 including land, buildings, and equipment in the 1930s.[1] For decades, there had been appeals for some assistance in amalgamating the small old factories into fewer medium-sized ones insulated to operate year-round, scaled for truck deliveries, and equipped with modern refrigeration. A survey before World War I found that only 48 of the 950 cheese factories in Eastern Ontario had refrigerated curing rooms, and only 21 of the 211 factories left in Western Ontario had them.[2] However, the factories were left the way they were until 1939, when cheese was once again needed to feed the fighting troops. By then, the number of cheese factories had shrunk by half. But at least during the war, prices were stable again.

The Master Craftsmen

Financially, cheesemaking was little more than "an existence." But it was still a craft, and that's what many of the cheesemakers focussed on — the part they could still take pride in and have some control over.

"From the beginning," Fred Day remembers, "show cheese was special. You knew your milk; you knew your patrons, the ones that were always good. So you'd pick out your 12,000 pounds — today, you can't do it the same; because today you have no control."

Ten miles up the road at Molesworth, Russ Martin would be doing the same thing making up a batch of show cheese for June, July, and August. "If you had room, why you'd switch the milk into the one vat, and the ordinary milk into the other, and then we'd give it special attention all the way, y'know, to make sure it was coming along at the right speed and so on."

Orchestrating the elements of heat, bacteria, rennet, and time, each cheesemaker tried to salt the curd to set the ferment at just the right point of acid build-up to set off the right free-fall sequence of aging in the curing room. As cheese ages, from 60 days for mild cheddar through to a year and more for strong old cheddar, enzymes break down the fatty acids and protein in the cheese. The chains of fatty acids become free fatty acids, which combine with the alcohol left from the fermenting process. This produces cheddar's distinctive aroma, pungent enough in old raw-milk cheddar to almost burn the back of the throat. The distinctive flavour of Ontario cheddar comes through when milk protein is broken down through protease enzymes. Government and industry have spent a lot of money trying to speed the aging process through special bacteria cultures, trying to replicate the full-bodied flavour of old cheese through artificial enzyme supplements, Dr. Arthur Hill reports. But so far, nothing can beat, or even equal, the results of simply leaving cheese to age naturally, in its own time, on its own terms.

That is what these craftsmen did. Beyond turning the cheeses every other day in the curing room, they ignored them and carried on with their daily business. They would have their regular monthly meetings to talk about the trouble this one was having with a slow vat (probably old culture or poor rennet) or gassy curd (something not too clean in the milk). From June through August, they also played a lot of baseball, one cheesemakers' association against another or in local community tournaments. At the end of the summer, some of the Perth County cheesemakers had a ritual of helping each other choose which cheeses to finish for showing. In the cool of each other's curing room, each pushed his metal cheese tryer into the top

Fred Day (right) and colleague on the steps of the Britton Cheese Factory while working for master cheesemaker Les Adair, Jack Bain's successor.

Fred Day (right) and assistant showing prizes won in 1949 at a local Agricultural Society cheesemaking competition — saucepan, lamp, and alarm clock.

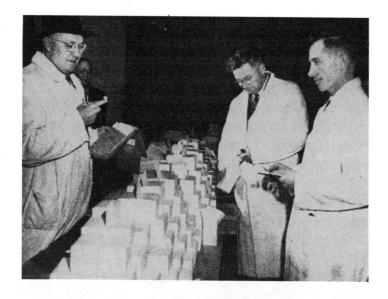

Judging butter and cheese at the 80th annual Western Ontario Dairyman's Association Convention, 1947.

of a cheese, turned the semi-cylindrical shaft 180 degrees, then pulled it out with what they called a "plug" of cheese lodged in the metal groove.

Cheese is judged on the basis of its texture, the closeness of the curd, the overall look, and, finally, the flavour.

After examining the plug for texture, cheesemakers like Fred Day and his friends Russ Martin and Les Adair (who took over the Britton factory in 1941 when Jack Bain went to work for the government) took a piece and bent it. A good plug should bend like a piece of hard plastic, but not break. Next, they rubbed a bit between their thumb and fingers, then brought it up to their noses. The flavour, judged entirely by the smell, should be clean and clear, though also pungent.

Once they'd given each other the benefit of their collective judgment on which cheeses each should finish for showing, then it was all-out competition. Competition in the heyday of the cheese shows was so close that a prize could be won or lost just by how well you dressed your finished cheese.

Fred Day remembers it was a lot of work. First he stripped off the cloth bandage and went over each of his 90-pound cheeses looking for mould or any other imperfection. He chipped this out with his pocketknife. Then he washed the surface with hot water, the heat helping to smooth out the holes and make it easier to slip on a new cheesecloth bandage:

And that seam, you gotta get that straight. You're allowed five points for finish, see? And that's one way you can help yourself. And you take your ruler and your level and you measure it. You'd take your thumb and get it smoothed level to the top, and then you'd cut around the top. I used to get Edith to do that; she was steadier with the scissors than I was. And then it goes in and out of the press a few times. It takes a few times to get all the holes smoothed out. I'd come into the house and set the alarm for an hour and get up and take them out of the presses, and finish 'em.

It wasn't any fun making show cheese. You lose a lot of sleep time. . . . But you felt real good when you saw in the paper where you'd done some winnings. This Tommy Aikins was a hard man to beat. One year him and I, he had a first there in June coloured, and I had the first in June white, and he had first in July coloured, and I had second in July coloured. We went to Dairy School together in 1941.

At the 1948 Listowel Fall Fair, Fred Day won a bedside lamp, a wind-up clock, and a small, stainless steel cooking pot. However, at the Western and Eastern Ontario Dairymen's shows in London and Brockville, at the Royal Winter Fair in Toronto, and the British Empire Show at Belleville, the prizes were cash money: $25 and more sometimes. Fred Day won his share over

Judging cheese at the Canadian National Exhibition, 1895 (top), and at the Eastern Ontario Dairymen's Association Cheese Competition and Show, Brockville, 1948 (below).

the years, taking the Grand Champion at The Royal in 1948 and placing second at The British Empire Show in 1949. So did Russ Martin and Les Adair.

"It was good advertising too. And the prize money helped pay the expenses. But mostly it was the satisfaction," Fred concluded.

The three friends travelled to the shows together, first by train and later by car. Once there, they'd find their own cheeses and check they were displayed well. There were thousands of cheeses at the largest competitions such as the British Empire Championship at Belleville. They were exhibited in the ball room of the Quinte Hotel, set out on linen table cloths with vases of flowers tastefully placed among them. They put in time until the evening awards banquet by touring the hospitality suites of the major suppliers, attending the odd lecture on bacteriology or new technology, and visiting around from room to room.

It seemed everyone came to these events: cheese buyers like Eardley Wright from Kraft, Bill Cooke from Black Diamond, and Gordon Henry from Canada Packers; cheesemakers who'd gone on to work as government graders, like Donald Menzies of Molesworth, or as government inspector-instructors like Jack Bain, dairy school instructors such as Don Irvine, suppliers such as Jack Beaton and, from all over the province, cheesemakers young and old.

Claude Flood used to go to Belleville and Brockville as cheesemaker and president of his local cheesemakers' association. "I always figured I was mingling with the best cheesemakers and I was always learning something," he said.

They came for the judging. They stayed for the stories.

"Cheesemakers are like a lodge," Fred Day told me. "They say that when a bunch of farmers get together, they'll talk horses till midnight, then they'll go to bed. But a bunch of cheesemakers, they'll talk till four in the morning."

There were stories about ornery patrons, safely distanced for the moment. There were also the legends: tales of standing up to the likes of the CPR with its fixed, high freight rates for hauling cheese to Montreal. John Fraser told the story that when his father added truck hauling to cheese-boxing, weighing, storing, and other services in the cheese business, the railway company threatened to build a local cold storage and drive him out of business.

"You may be long, but I'm wide," Neil was reputed to have told the company representative who'd dropped by to bully him a little.

There were stories about larger developments in the cheese business: for instance, who got the contracts to supply cheese for the war effort. Gordon Henry had a story about Joseph Flavelle, founding partner of Canada Packers, who used his connections in the Imperial War Office in London to corner the market on supplying the war office with pork.[1]

Over the years, these stories were told more and more simply as stories, personal stories. They weren't to make a point on which the cheesemakers should take a united stand. By the 1930s, cheddar cheese accounted for only 19 per cent of the milk produced in Ontario,[2] though there were still 632 cheese factories plus 46 combined cheese plants and creameries across the province.[3] Alex McClaren and D.M. McPherson were the last generation of cheese men to gain the clout of political office. Now even their associations had lost most of their original influence. They were eclipsed by the Whole-Milk Producers' Association and the Ontario Concentrated Milk Producers' Association. Equally important, they were eclipsed on the manufacturing side by the milk-powder manufacturers' association, the concentrated milk processors' and their umbrella organizations, the Ontario Dairy Products Manufacturers, and the National Dairy Council, which were dominated by big dairies, often American branch plants. Furthermore, the leaders of these organizations were businessmen like S.B. Trainor of Silverwoods. When the government worked with the dairy industry now, they worked most easily with these groups and these men of business. They talked the same language and worked with their heads, not their hands and heads united organically in the context of daily craftsmanship.

Wes Krotz, Jack Bain, and Fred Day carried on with the Western Ontario Dairymen's Association, each taking a turn as president and secretary-treasurer, doing what they could in a diminishing sphere of influence.

PART THREE
Decline and Neglect

Borden Condenser
Tillsonburg, Ontario

Prologue

May 8, 1945: The war had dragged on so long it was like a distant drone to Doug Rowe, the cheesemaker at Hoard Station. His wife Emma's brothers were overseas, and he was used to worrying about them, bracing himself for telegrams. Like his brother Delbert, Doug had been exempted from the draft by the necessity of making cheese — something he'd been doing since he was a boy. He'd been scrupulous in filling his requisition orders, though he knew some who sent more cheese on paper than in fact and sold the difference as bootleg. He was a quiet, serious young man with a pale thin face framed in jet-black hair. When the milk in the cheese vats had warmed to 86° F and his nose detected just the right hint of lactic acid, he added rennet to set the curd. Then he heard a shouting commotion and rushed to the door.

A man was running down the middle of the gravel road swinging a cow bell in one hand and a Union Jack in the other. He was yelling at the top of his lungs: "The war is over; come on, come on. The war is over; come on, come on."

His voice cracked with emotion, but he kept on yelling. He flailed the light spring air with the incredible news. "The war is over; come on, come on."

The vats had set and Doug had to cut the curd. So Emma went, and Doug kept running back and forth from the cheese vats to the screened front door. Everywhere he looked, people were running, drawn by instinct to the logical meeting spot: the World War I Cenotaph in the centre of the village in the gently hollowed landscape of Hastings County in Central Ontario. There women and men wept openly for those who could now come home and those who never would. The minister arrived out of breath and offered a prayer. Then someone started "hip-hip hooray." It grew so loud the words carried all the way up the road to the cheese factory.

When the sound died away, Doug wiped his eyes and carried on with his work as though everything had gone back to normal.

But everything had changed. Forty per cent of Canada's adult male population (and a significant fraction of its women) had served overseas.[1] In the summer of 1946, one million men and 50,000 women came home — home to a country transformed into an urban industrial power with the underpinnings of a welfare state well in place.[2] The federal bureaucracy had totalled 46,000 employees in 1939. It had grown to 116,000 by 1945.[3]

A new Ministry of Veterans' Affairs offered tuition assistance, and in Ontario nearly 13,000 veterans grabbed the chance at higher education.[4] A National Housing Act offered assistance in housing, and by 1947, 19,000 loans for new homes had been approved.[5] C.D. Howe, who had rationalized Canadian industry into 28 Crown corporations as Minister of Munitions and Supply during the war, became the minister responsible for Reconstruction, promising jobs and steady wages. As well, there was unemployment insurance, introduced in 1942. And a third new department, the Ministry of Health and Welfare, launched in 1944, administered a national family allowance as part of a broad program of social welfare.[6]

Financing this was a set of employment-generating manufacturing industries plus a new wave of staples exports, including hydroelectric power from Ontario and Quebec and Western oil and gas, launched at Leduc, Alberta, in 1947, by Imperial Oil. In Ontario and Western Quebec, through which Allied war efforts had been channelled via branch plants of many American companies, the war had boosted industrialization. Canada's steel-making capacity was now 50 per cent greater than at the start of the war. Canadian factories were making aircraft, diesel engines, synthetic rubber, plastics, and electronic equipment; none of these were made at the start of the war.[7]

Now the newly formed Ontario Ministry of Planning and Development air-lifted 10,000 skilled British workers and their families to help retool manufacturing from military supplies to consumer products. By 1949, the value of Ontario manufacturing products was up 50 per cent over 1945 levels. Salaries were up by 50 per cent as well, for a work week which had dropped from 50 to 41 hours.[8]

In politics, George Drew retooled the federal Conservatives into the "Progressive" Conservatives, with a social-reform platform geared to people as consumers and individuals, no longer as groups defined by class and differing visions of society.[9] It was the beginning of brokerage politics, with "special-interest" groups and "protest" groups mediated by bureaucrats, although the dialogue was dominated by urban big business. By 1963, no political party could hope to gain office, or remain there for any length of time, without the support of big business. Equally important, the rural vote alone was no longer sufficient to counter or even significantly challenge its position.[10]

Internally, the local elites were shifting allegiance. During the war, Canada had moved out of the orbit of Britain and the disintegrating British Empire and into the sphere of the United States. Prime Minister Mackenzie King had rebuffed offers to join an alliance of ex-colonial commonwealth countries in favour of closer ties with the U.S.[11] Under the prime ministership of former Washington ambassador "Mike" Pearson, the tilt toward the U.S. increased. It was understood that to chart too independent a course or to criticize U.S. economic domination of Canada was to undermine the American-led fight against communism.[12]

The shift from Britain to the United States showed up dramatically in trade. While in 1938, Britain had taken 41 per cent of Canada's exports and the U.S.A. 33 per cent, by 1946, the proportions were reversed. By 1957, the U.S.A. was absorbing 59 per cent of Canada's exports (mostly energy and minerals), and the U.K. only 15 per cent. Furthermore Britain, which had supplied 60 per cent of Canada's imports in 1872, was supplying only 18 per cent by the outbreak of the war and 9 per cent by 1957, whereas the U.S.A., which had supplied 32 per cent of Canada's imports in 1872, was supplying 63 per cent in 1938 and 71 per cent by 1957.[13]

The integration and related dependency went beyond trade. It also included technological, managerial, and capital dependency as American companies came to control 43 per cent of Canadian manufacturing and 52 per cent of mining and smelting by 1957.[14] (Tight Canadian monetary policies at least contributed to the financial dependency. With interest rates higher in Canada than in the U.S.A. through much of the 1950s, American money filled the gap[15]. However, this took the form of "direct" investment, as branches of American parent companies. These branches were subordinate to the parent firm and forced to depend on them for technology and management services. They were also deliberately limited in scale, to serve and supply the Canadian domestic market only.)

The pattern was clearest in areas where Americans had pioneered technologies and industries — such as cars and trucks, electric tools, and appliances. But it also spread into areas where local companies had once been strong, including the export market. In the dairy industry, Borden's, Beatrice Foods, Carnation, and Kraft were a dominant presence both in Quebec and Ontario by the late 1940s. In 1947, Borden's, Silverwoods, and Dominion Dairies controlled 40 per cent of all milk products handled by milk distributors in Ontario.[16] An Ontario Royal Commission noted that this was "a tendency that requires watchful attention" and left it at that.[17]

Two federal royal commissions sounded the alarm on foreign control: one, chaired by Vincent Massey in 1950, and another, chaired by Walter Gordon in 1957. But nothing was done, at least partly because popular opinion remained largely indifferent to the problem — until the late 1960s when protests against American imperialism were heard.

In Ontario during the 1950s, Premier Leslie Frost cultivated a reassuring public image as "Old Man Ontario" whose window on the world was a barbershop in small-town Lindsay. Meanwhile, he continued George Drew's work of consolidating and expanding manufacturing and resource industries and catering to voters as members of a modern welfare state. He welcomed American investment, tolerating foreign control as the price of steady employment and the tax dollars essential for popular social services.[18] Continuing the Tory tradition of public investment in the infrastructure for development, Frost backed the St. Lawrence Seaway project, a joint Canada-U.S.A. power and navigation system. At the opening of the Seaway on 27 June, 1959, attended by President Eisenhower as well as Queen Elizabeth II, a commemorative painting was presented to Her Majesty depicting the old Ontario farms, villages, and bushland that had been displaced by the construction. The painting was the work of Stuart McCormick, son of the last stone mason in Glengarry County.[19] Six thousand people lost their homes when the 23 billion cubic feet of water from Lake Ontario was released into the seaway that day.[20]

Before the war, small-town Ontario had served as a bridge between the urban and rural populations. Stone masons, blacksmiths, harness and carriage makers lived there, along with makers of cheese and butter, furniture, and farm implements. By contributing to the farm community, they helped to sustain it. But in the post-war period, many of these industries disappeared. They were replaced by more modern, city-oriented enterprises: branch plants that manufactured or simply assembled outboard motors, washing machines, fridges, stoves, and television sets. By 1961, 90 per cent of Ontario's work force was in manufacturing. Over 75 per cent of the population was classed as "urban," while less than 10 per cent lived on farms. In Toronto alone, suburban expansion swallowed up the previously self-contained little towns of Leaside, Mimico, New Toronto, and Weston, the villages of Forest Hill, Long Branch, and Swansea, and the townships of East York, North York, Etobicoke, and Scarborough.[21]

The suburbs were the birthplace of post-war Ontario. Here a generation of men and women who had lost their teen years to the Depression and their 20s to the war staked out their claim first to security and then to comfort and the good life. The baby-boom generation was raised here — people like myself. We grew up on streets called Elm, Maple, or Birch, surrounded by lawn mowers, snow blowers, televisions, and cars. The cars were bought on credit and traded in every four or five years.

More than anything else, economists concluded later, consumerism fuelled the post-war economy and forestalled the slump many had predicted with the winding down of war. Consumerism consisted of producing goods primarily for them to be consumed and buying them for the same purpose. It was geared to the suburban family. It was promoted through the mass marketing techniques of television advertising and delivered through modern supermarkets and shopping centres.

In the countryside, the post-war period was a time of decay and wrenching readjustment. Between 1941 and 1956, two-and-a-half million acres of Ontario farmland were abandoned. Two-thirds of the farms were 60 acres or less, generally small frame buildings often without electricity, refrigeration, or indoor plumbing. Forty-two per cent were at least partly original log houses. A quarter were on roads which had themselves been abandoned or were open only in the summer.[22]

The local schools were condemned as "an educational slum," and the 1,423 locally autonomous rural school boards were replaced by 248 school districts regulated out of Toronto.[23]

While farm incomes lagged through the 1930s and 1940s, farm machinery costs nearly doubled between 1937 and 1947 as farmers switched from horses to tractors and the implements designed to be pulled by them. By 1958, tractors outnumbered horses on Ontario farms for the first time.[24] To make ends meet, farmers and their sons went out to work on the Seaway and other post-war building projects. Daughters were sent to the city to work as store clerks and domestic help in the mansions of Rosedale and Westmount.

Once-famous breeders of draft and carriage horses turned to the brood-mare business. Their splendid Percherons and Hackneys were valuable now only for the urine they produced while pregnant. It was shipped to Montreal and Toronto, where branch plants of U.S. pharmaceutical companies extracted estrogen hormones for the manufacture of women's face creams. The colts were shot at birth, the fillies raised solely for service in the brood-mare business.

Outside Vankleek Hill, Mary McKinnon, living alone on the family farm, milked her one Jersey cow morning and evening, loaded the milk can onto the wooden wagon she'd had since she was a girl, and hauled the milk down the road to the Aberdeen Cheese Factory, managed by Neil Fraser's son John.

It was a time when the cheddar cheese business, always struggling, approached near-total collapse. Between 1941 and 1956, 412 cheese factories went out of business across the province. In Western and Central Ontario, 111 factories disappeared, leaving only 31. In Eastern Ontario, 301 closed or switched over to butter, leaving 113. Most factories that closed were small, producing less than 50 tons of cheese a year.[25] These likely lacked insulation and modern conveniences and still had their original equipment, labour-intensive machinery run by conveyor belt off a much-repaired steam boiler. They were often on roads which themselves were closed or, at best, passable only in the summer. Many of these factories had been neglected so long it made no sense to even attempt renovations. They were simply closed and converted to storage. A few went up in what came to be known as an "insurance fire," the slow-moving type that allowed the cheesemaker time to get most if not all of his belongings to safety.[26] A few others were closed as part of the long-overdue Cheese Factory Improvement Program, launched in 1939, which payed half the cost of modernizing cheesemaking facilities by replacing at least two old cheese factories with a larger, refrigerated one.

These were small signs of optimism in an otherwise depressed environment.

In 1955, cheesemakers were still making only between $ 2,000 and $3,316 a year for a work week ranging from 60 to 80 hours and six or even seven days a week.[27] In 1961, the federal Agricultural Rehabilitation and Development Program actually paid people to move off the land into towns and cities.[28]

That same year, the hours of the Ontario legislature were quietly amended. The House would no longer adjourn for spring seeding, but carry on, in step with expanding government business and government bureaucracy. John Robarts replaced "Old Man Ontario" Leslie Frost as premier and declared, "This is the era of the management man, and I am a management man."[29]

Brought to You by . . . the Makers of Processed Cheese

Kraft had done well through the war. Canadian sales almost doubled, from $8 million in 1939 to $14 million by 1945,[1] in part through government requisitions of its processed cheese for the armed forces.[2] Kraft also became one of the first big advertisers in the electronic media. In the 1940s, it sponsored the *Bing Crosby Show* (called "The Kraft Music Hall") on radio. Then, when television came along in the 1950s, it sponsored the *Perry Como Show, Walt Disney Presents*, and the *Red River Jamboree*. On the French network, it sponsored *Cinema Kraft*.[3]

By 1973, Kraft was the largest single advertiser in Canadian magazines, and, with General Foods, the largest advertiser on television.[4]

Tom Quinn built a career on media marketing and, at the end of it, still marvelled how the media had changed marketing from simply getting the goods to market to creating a desire for them in the first place. Ottawa-born and educated, his first job after the war was as one of Kraft's 1,000-plus travelling salesmen. His job was to turn the images implanted through advertising into sales at the Ottawa and area stores on his sales beat. He was helped by a line

A jar of Millar's Canadian (Ingersoll) "Paragon" brand processed cheese.

Ingersoll Packing Co. Ltd. advertisement, 1918.

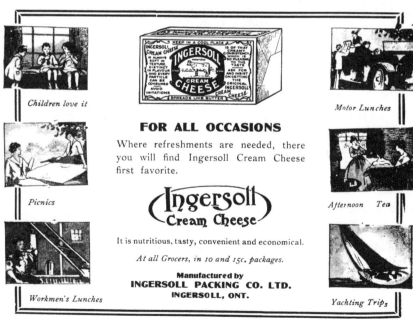

Children love it

Picnics

Workmen's Lunches

FOR ALL OCCASIONS

Where refreshments are needed, there you will find Ingersoll Cream Cheese first favorite.

Ingersoll Cream Cheese

It is nutritious, tasty, convenient and economical.

At all Grocers, in 10 and 15c. packages.

Manufactured by
INGERSOLL PACKING CO. LTD.
INGERSOLL, ONT.

Motor Lunches

Afternoon Tea

Yachting Trips

of processed cheeses developed and tested in the U.S. that positively sparkled with new ideas like "convenience" — and consumers wanted convenience. (The company had discovered this through scientific market testing.) There was Velveeta, a staple in kids' lunches through the 1950s; Cheese Whiz, introduced at the end of the decade; and cheese slices, which went to school in millions, if not billions, of kids' sandwiches across a tuned-in North America through the 1960s, 1970s and 1980s.

Quinn found a ready audience in local store managers itching with post-war cabin fever. With a growing consumer economy, they were open to his suggestions. They were especially open once the Kraft salesman showed them that cheese didn't have to mean the chronically small and marginal returns on 90-pound rounds of cheddar which grocers traditionally kept in the meat counter and which housewives normally bought only to accompany apple pie. Traditionally, too, the best Ontario cheddar was reserved for the British export market, with the slightly inferior stuff dumped on the local market. Thus, while Ontario cheddar was praised internationally, it had a low reputation at home.[5]

Kraft was selling processed cheese. This was different.

An Ingersoll businessman, Dippey (T.D.) Millar, created what is thought to have been the first processed cheese in the 1870s. This was a "cold pack" type that involved the blending of cheddars ranging from young to as much as ten years old. He packaged and sold this in opaque jars as "Millar's Royal Paragon" cheese, with pictures of medals he'd won at international cheese shows in London and Amsterdam.[6]

Shortly after he died in 1894, his nephew sold the business to the English-based cheese and importing firm of J.L. Grant and Co.[7] Meanwhile, one of Millar's employees, Alex McLaren, developed his own brand of processed cheese in 1897.[8] Calling it "McLaren's Imperial," he marketed it through his highly successful cheese-exporting business, including in the U.S. through a branch office in Detroit. In 1921, he sold the business to James Lewis Kraft of Chicago who, in turn, launched his Canadian subsidiary, Kraft-McLaren Cheese Co. of Canada, that same year.[9]

James Kraft is thought to have pioneered the hot version of pasteurized processed cheese. Born in 1874 on a farm at Stevensville, Ontario, Kraft's first job was clerking at Ferguson's General Store in Fort Erie. He noticed that no self-respecting housewife would buy cheese without first sampling it, using crackers in a cracker barrel on the counter where the cheese was kept, "for, no matter how wholesome it was when it left the manufacturer, it often reached the market in a state of extinct virtue," Kraft declared, according to a biographical sketch of his early days. "James L. Kraft felt a better and more economical way to merchandise cheese could be

found . . . and felt that destiny had marked him a maker of cheese that would perish not."[10]

Kraft went to Buffalo, where he took a short business course. In 1903 he moved to Chicago, feeling this was the best spot from which to launch a business. The business started with a double boiler for heating and blending cheddar cheese which he bought on credit from a local wholesaler, plus a rented wagon and a horse called Paddy for selling his product to local grocers. In 1916, he successfully patented his formula for processed cheese, shutting down would-be competitors by obliging any to pay him a royalty, though he later made an agreement with Borden's to use certain emulsifiers in his recipe, which were said to have "completed the development of the hot pack process" of making processed cheese.[11]

Kraft supplied the armed forces with tins of processed cheese during World War I. Then, after buying out McLaren's, he continued his Canadian expansions, using McLaren Imperial's facilities in Montreal and marketing a five-pound loaf of pasteurized processed cheese in the urban consumer market.[12] In the U.S., his expansions took the form of diversification into other lines of food. In the 1920s, he bought one of the biggest salad-dressing firms in the country, plus five others in the Southern and Eastern states. Eventually, he put the Kraft label on over 200 different food products.[13]

Kraft's Canadian expansions continued

through the Second World War. While enlarging his supply contracts with the federal government, he gained control over several cheese factories in Quebec and Ontario, principally through exclusive supply contracts. He renamed the company from Kraft Cheese to simply Kraft Foods after the war, preparatory to introducing the next string of products: Parkay Margarine, launched in 1949, Kraft Caramels in 1950, Kraft Peanut Butter, and so on.

In 1955, Kraft introduced its own name and label for Ontario cheddar cheese: Kraft's own "Cracker Barrel" Cheese.[14] Tom Quinn's job was to move these cheeses into people's shopping carts, as he explains:

We had lots of things. Getting the product off the shelves and putting it into jumble displays where people would go and mess with it, and pick it up. . . . We had numbers and figures that we worked with — product sold from these displays versus off the shelf, and the increase in sales, they were phenomenal. Fifty per cent more the store would sell in a week if they would move it off the shelf.

And in those days, they had a little display unit in front of each check-out counter, and the thing to do was to sell that manager to get those display units for a weekend. And this means that as she goes by, the last thing she saw was that, and if the product was well advertised, which it was, and it triggered her memory, why she'd maybe pick it up and put it in her basket.

The Kraft promotions were augmented by industry projects such as the "Cheese Festival" sponsored by the National Dairy Council, in which Kraft had been active since the 1920s. Together, these efforts helped boost per-capita cheese consumption to a record high of nearly 10 pounds per capita by 1967.[15] They also implanted a new name and taste for cheese in the public mind. This was the uniform, bland taste of processed cheese, not the distinctive sharpness of aged Ontario cheddar, consumption of which stagnated and even slumped.

Tom Quinn eventually became President of Kraft Foods (Canada) Ltd. in Montreal. White haired and rosy cheeked, he sat in his office in the months prior to his retirement and smiled as he concluded: "We at Kraft are experts at merchandising. If we did anything right, it was merchandising and advertising. We created the demand."

A Blow to the British Connection

In 1949, Doug Rowe finally managed to buy his own cheese factory, "a run-down rickety old plant" just outside Warkworth in Hastings County. He borrowed money from a farmer he knew at Hoard Station who wrote out the terms ($4,000 at 5 per cent) on a strip of brown paper and posted it on a nail inside the milk shed:

The factory was just lumber on the inside, shingles on the outside, and it shook when the engine was going. I mean, it was still sitting on posts. And there were rats. So we started fixing it up. We put in a foundation underneath, and put in a new floor, and then we started to get modern. We got this here travelling agitator that went up and down the vat. And you could put forkers on after the whey was drew off and fork the curd instead of doing it all by hand — for to work the moisture out of it.

Still, it was "just an existence," and a poor one at that. Because the factory was uninsulated, he was forced to close it from January through March, when he'd cut wood out in the bush for a paltry 15 cents a cord. "I've cut enough wood for 15 cents a cord," he told me years later.

One day in 1950, Jack Bain dropped in. "He was a friend to everyone; I knew him well," Doug told me. The former cheesemaker was chief cheese instructor for all Western and Central Ontario now, and he was encouraging small cheesemakers to take advantage of the federal Cheese Factory Improvement Program. In 1947, the Wells Royal Commission on Milk reported that all but two of the 50 amalgamations to date had occurred in Quebec. Of the two Ontario projects, one involved Kraft, the other Aults, which sold most of its cheese to Kraft.[1]

Indirectly, Kraft was one of the main beneficiaries of the program, in what quickly became its main arrangement for securing cheese supplies. Buyer agents would approach small farmer-owned cheese factories, offering annual supply contracts as leverage for financing their half of the amalgamation project. They'd tell them what kind of equipment would help them make cheese to Kraft specifications — mostly American technology by this time. This included square cheese hoops for making 40-pound blocks of cheese, which Kraft re-worked into processed cheese or aged and repackaged with the Cracker Barrel label. The Kraft people not only signed supply contracts with the new plant, they also paid a two-cent-a-pound premium until the plants had paid off their loans. During the war years, most of Kraft's expansion in Canada was along these lines, and

WARKWORTH CHEESE COUNTRY

Warkworth Cheese House.

Doug and Emma Rowe,
Warkworth, Ontario.

principally among the farmer-owned cooperatives in Quebec. In the area of Lac St. Jean alone, something like 30 factories were amalgamated into 10. Another cluster of amalgamations occurred up river near Granby, where the Agricole Cooperative de Granby would become the largest dairy processing company in Canada. From the beginning it made all of its cheese under contract for Kraft.

Although fieldmen like Jack Bain made a point of promoting the amalgamation program, getting cheesemakers into it wasn't easy. The program required that cheese-factory owners build the new plant and equip it with refrigeration, etc., entirely on their own first. Only when it was finished and its operating licence issued would the government contribute its half of the approved construction costs. Furthermore, all building plans had to be submitted in duplicate and include tenders from possible suppliers of materials and equipment. Finally, since the program was intended to encourage consolidation as well as modernization, applicants had to have bought out at least one other local cheese factory so that the new building would replace two old ones. It required a lot of money up front.

Doug Rowe had a couple of hundred dollars in Victory Bonds, but that was it. The local bank, a branch of the Royal, concentrated on short-term credit at high interest rates. So Doug went to see another old neighbour. "You see," he told me, "farmers weren't in such a hurry for to get their money back, as long as they got their interest."

To get the rest, Jack Bain sent him to see the newly created Ontario Development Corporation. As Doug recalls,

There was no office around here, so I had to go way down to Toronto to see them. And, oh, all the things they wanted to know and one thing and another. About collateral. I said I didn't have any. They asked me if I had any machinery, a truck and so on. Well, yes. Why, you have all kinds of collateral, they said.

In 1952 the factory went up as approved. Doug Rowe got his licence to operate and a cheque from the amalgamation program. In his first year, he made three times the volume of the old factory.

Then the bottom fell out of the cheddar cheese market. In 1952, Britain cut off all cheddar cheese imports as a post-war austerity measure. In fact, by the post-war period, barely 50 per cent of Canada's cheese was being exported, compared with 80 per cent in the 1920s. Canada's share of Britain's cheese market had slipped from the dominant position it had enjoyed in the late 1800s to only 12 per cent of the market by 1947.[2] Still, most independent and farmer-owned cheese factories making traditional raw-milk or heat-treated cheddar regarded the British market as the pillar of their existence. To a certain extent they were living remnants of the British imperial period. Canadian, and particularly Ontario, cheddar continued to grace the windows of Sainsbury's and other fine food shops in London. Not only that, it sold for as much as 25 per cent more than the price paid for competing cheese from, for instance, New Zealand.

When the British government cut off cheese imports, the effect was staggering. Fifty-five cheese factories closed in one season, and an additional 50 shut down the following year.[3] Cheddar output dropped from 66 million pounds to 51 million as farmers frantically sought other markets for their milk.

It was a time when the cheese interests should have spoken up with one united voice. Instead there were three: the traditional craftsmen associated with the county cheesemakers' associations and the Dairymen's Association of Western Ontario; the farmer-patrons associated with farmer-owned cooperative cheese factories which had traditionally been strongest in East-Central Ontario; and the more entrepreneurial group of private owners who associated themselves with the bigger dairy interests associated with the National Dairy Council, many of whom lived in Eastern Ontario.

At a meeting of the Dairymen's Association of Western Ontario in London, oldtimers like Jack Bain and Wes Krotz advocated a revival of the cheese mammoths as a device for finding new markets for cheddar both across Canada and in the United States. In Belleville, farmer-directors of the Ontario Cheese Producers Association decided to lobby for government assistance. A delegation took the train to Toronto to plead for a subsidy on cheese prices under the Agricultural Cooperative Marketing Act.

Doug Rowe didn't attend either of those meetings. Getting to the first was probably a problem of distance. As for the second, because he was a factory owner, he didn't fit the Cheese Producers' mould. Instead, he accepted an invitation from John Fraser of Vankleek Hill to join the Ontario Cheese Manufacturers' Association. Formed in 1950 with a membership including Eardley Wright of Kraft and Sam Ault of Winchester, the association decided to lobby Ottawa.[4] They appealed to federal Agriculture Minister Jimmy Gardiner and Prime Minister Louis St. Laurent to reinstate the support-price subsidy for cheese which had been discontinued in 1947.[5]

The lobbying efforts brought some short-term relief. They also drew the attention of two levels of government to the problems of the Ontario cheese industry: problems of obsolete facilities, questionable sanitary measures, and amateurish business practices. Many of these were a function of the industry's chronic impoverishment and the related neglect of marketing issues. But the government would focus on the symptoms rather than the root problems.

Meanwhile, as Ontario's cheesemakers turned from the export to the local home market, they found that the market was already occupied. The 50 per cent of Canadian cheese production which already flowed into the domestic market was marketed so overwhelmingly under the Kraft label that, for many Canadians, cheese meant Kraft just as movies meant Hollywood and soft drinks meant Coke.

In the spring of 1955, Doug Rowe signed a contract to make cheese for Kraft and considered himself lucky to do so.

Forced March to Modern Times

In 1952, the federal and provincial governments decided to help market Ontario cheddar. They co-sponsored some exports to the U.S., hoping sales there might replace the moribund British trade. The Americans blocked some of the shipments at the border, however, on account of what the Canadians called "extraneous matter" and the Americans called simply "filth." Immediately, the provincial department of agriculture instructed its field staff to enforce new regulations rigorously, requiring screens in cheese factory windows and so on. In an effort to reduce sediment, the government arranged for testing to be done at the Guelph Dairy School and partially linked the two-cent premium for Grade A export cheese, which the federal government had been paying since 1939, to the production of clean and sediment-free cheese.[1]

The sediment problems were soon cleaned up; however, other problems conspired to get worse. In November 1953, T.B. Cooper, quality-control manager for Kraft, wrote to Ontario's director of dairying (C.E. Lackner) complaining about fly-control practices in cheese factories — or rather, the lack thereof:

Killing flies inside the plant, particularly with DDT which brings on a slow death, is bound to result in a goodly number falling into the product when they are finally overcome by the effects of the insecticide. We just have to work out ways and means of keeping them out of the plants.

In February 1954, Cooper sent Lackner another letter, forwarding a customer's complaint about a piece of cheese "which was very badly contaminated with dead flies." He went on to report from his field staff that "although a great number of factories were complying in some manner with your new Ontario regulations, they are not backing this up. . . . In many instances we found doors wide open so that flies came in and were trapped in the make room, so that there were actually far more present than there would have been had there been no screens in the windows."[2]

Albert Ouellette, a cheesemaker from Manitoba hired by Kraft in 1955 to supervise the company's field staff, remembered those days even after he'd retired:

Extraneous matter in cheese was just horrible. There was anything from pocket watches to rings to coins. Flies was the worst. . . . There used to be a saying, "Don't buy cheese made Christmas Eve" because you could find almost anything in it. Once there was half a bottle of liquor in a 90-pound round. Somebody had come in, and they'd hid the bottle in one of the hoops and put the curd in around it and then forgotten it. Oh, you could find all kinds of things.[3]

The government's complaints file grew thicker. C.E. Lackner received a letter forwarded from Loblaws written by a Mrs. Betty Angell of Uxbridge, Ontario, on April 3:

On Saturday, March 20, I purchased a piece of wrapped red cheese from your store and found a dead fly in same.

Today I purchased a piece of wrapped yellow cheddar cheese, and found a dead fly in this piece. The first occasion I passed as "just one of those things." But this is going too far.[4]

That summer, Lackner's office received word that a Loblaw's customer from Eastern Ontario was in the hospital with a pin in her throat. The cheese she'd been eating at the time, with more pins still in it, had been forwarded to Toronto where the company's legal department was looking into the matter.

A meeting of the government's cheese quality advisory committee, chaired by Sam Ault, agreed that something had to be done to enforce government standards, especially in Central and Eastern Ontario. In 1951, Agriculture Minister Col. Tom Kennedy created the powerful new position of Dairy Commissioner and appointed Everett Biggs, the competent young agricultural representative in his riding. Biggs was raised on a Holstein farm in the Ottawa Valley, which delivered fluid milk to a dairy in the town of Pembroke.[5] He had interrupted his studies at the Ontario Agricultural College to serve overseas during the war. He returned as an army major, resuming his studies in 1945, the year George McLaughlin, another Holstein farmer, completed his studies at Guelph. The yearbooks show that, like McLaughlin, Ev Biggs was active in public speaking and the debating club, though he also enjoyed boxing. A year after graduating, he won a Rotary Club scholarship to go to England to study the workings of the newly established British Milk Marketing Board.

As Jim Baker explained to me, Biggs's first act as Dairy Commissioner was to streamline the nine pieces of legislation affecting Ontario dairying into the Milk Industry Act of 1954. This introduced a Sanitary Standards Code, integrating some of the old regulations — for instance, against milk adulteration — with new, tougher regulations on extraneous matter, testing for bacteria, butterfat, sediment , and comprehensive cheese factory inspections. A year or so after this code was introduced, Dairy Branch fieldmen were empowered to quarantine an offending plant if necessary. In 1957, a revised version of the act completed the regulatory consolidation and created the quasi-judicial Milk Industry Board to police the new regulatory environment.

At the same time, the Department of Labour stepped in to review and approve all blueprints for new cheese factories before an operating licence was issued. Traditionally, there was a joke around the field offices that the only rule governing construction of cheese factories was that "the walls shall be strong enough to support the roof." Politics kept government inspectors at bay, particularly where cheese factories were owned by farmers; farmer-patrons were an important voting bloc for local politicians.

"We figured the cheese industry was babied

too much," Jim Baker, former Dairy Commissioner, said years later in reference to what he saw as political coddling.

As well, the Department of Health started sending out its own inspectors, while municipal boards of health inspected farm dairies. Finally, there were inspectors from the federal Food and Drug Administration and provincial Water Resources Commission.

It was quite a change for cheesemakers, especially those who took pride in policing themselves. "We always figured we were the best inspectors," Doug Rowe said, aggrieved at having the roles reversed:

And you'd think everything was all right too, but they'd have this report made out, and this and that. A lot of them, now there's a lot of smart young people but some of them didn't use common sense. Why, some hung around just until they found something they could complain about — like a pipe with paint chipping off. And they'd mail this to me afterwards sort of thing. They could always come up with some little thing. You could never come up with a 100 per cent perfect report.

Some of the regulations actually created problems. For instance, under one regulation, Dairy Branch fieldmen told cheesemakers they couldn't send whey back home to the farmers in the same cans they used to deliver the milk. In

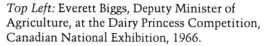

Top Left: Everett Biggs, Deputy Minister of Agriculture, at the Dairy Princess Competition, Canadian National Exhibition, 1966.

Top Right: Hector Arnold, President of the Ontario Cheese Producers, 1955–65.

Bottom: George McLaughlin, first Chairman of the Ontario Milk Marketing Board.

another, the Animal Husbandry Branch field-men told the farmers they couldn't keep pigs and cows in the same barn. Squeezed on both sides, many farmers got out of pigs and left their whey at the factory. There, yet another regulation said that whey disposal was the responsibility of whoever ran the place. The easiest solution was simply to dump the unwanted whey with the wash water into the creek beside which most cheese factories had been built. However, as Ontario's woodlands had been systematically cleared over the years, the water table had dropped considerably and, in the milk-souring days of high summer, many formerly free-flowing creeks were reduced to mere trickles between what became stagnant pools of whey.

The stench brought protests from the local villagers, many of whom were now commuting to factory jobs in nearby towns and had grown unaccustomed to strong barnyard smells. Their protests brought inspectors from the Water Resources Commission specializing in the new water-pollution regulatory business.

In the tranquil community of Prince Edward County, a sixth-generation Loyalist by the name of Gerald Ackerman was serving yet another term as president of the farmer-owned Black River Cheese Factory near Picton. A successful dairy and apple farmer, member of the board of the local school and the local church, Ackerman was confident of his ability to manage local affairs. Then one day, a Water Resources inspector — "just a young shaver of a lad in his 20s" — arrived and proceeded to do some water tests. "And he announced something about how it was oh-two-hundred upstream and oh-twenty-three downstream and a hundred and twenty-five opposite where this here whey shoots out into the crik, and he claimed that this was water pollution. So then he laid down the rule that we had to irrigate" by spreading the whey on open land and working it into the soil. When Ackerman pointed out that the cooperative didn't own any land, the inspector gestured to a field beside the factory. Ackerman replied,

"We can't buy that field because the fellow won't want to sell that field. Well," he says, "buy that field over there." And I told him, that's not for sale neither. So one word brought another, and I know that I got quite warm under the collar. We was on the bridge, and I felt like dumpin' him over into the crik. "Well," he says, "we'll just give you so many days and we'll come down and turn the key in the door." *He* was warm too, I guess.[6]

Ackerman wrote to Jack Bain, "a real prince of a chap," who by then was the head of the cheese division in the Dairy Branch. Bain investigated alternative methods of whey disposal and suggested that the government build a few centrally located whey-processing facilities across

Top: Black River Cheese Factory, near Picton, Ontario, 1902.

Bottom: Black River Cheese Co. Ltd., the only cheese factory remaining in Prince Edward County, 1993.

the province. They could be run as public utilities, available to any factory with whey for which it had no use. Bain spent the next 15 or so years trying to get this plan implemented, while the effects of the unresolved whey disposal problem hounded and harassed many factories out of existence.

At least it seemed like harassment to John Fraser at Vankleek Hill in Eastern Ontario, who had a string of about seven local cheese factories he either owned outright or managed or to which he sold supplies:

Inspection was crazy. You'd have them tripping over one another in here. You'd have one guy in here in the morning from Water Resources, saying you can't put any more whey up in that gravel pit. Sometimes I'd come home for lunch and there'd be three inspectors waiting for me here in the office.

It was just one thing after another, on our backs continuously. It was like a knife in your back all the time. There'd be Health and Welfare. And then Food and Drug would be in here checking up on screen doors — in January! Checking for flies in January! And then there'd be local inspectors. Whey disposal, that hurt us more than anything else. It beat a friend of mine. And it took down the whole industry. If they'd built a [whey] drying plant in the area, but they didn't want to get involved. But they'd be here anyway, inspectors.

Fraser sold a couple of factories to Carnation which had built a large milk-powder plant down the road at Alexandria in the early 1950s. Over the years, it had been drawing away more and more of John's patrons with promises of television sets and $1 a hundredweight more for year-round deliveries.

At Harrowsmith in Frontenac County, where Harold Kingston had bought his own factory and had expanded it through the Cheese Factory Improvement program, inspectors got at least as good as they gave. Once a pest-control inspector sent Kingston a directive to fix the gap between the door and the floor of his curing room. He'd used his flashlight to check this out one day when he stopped by the factory for inspection. As Harold tells the story:

Well of course he done that one day when I wasn't here. So the next day when he come along, why — I got quite a sassy letter from him, see? So when he come in, I said, "Where's your flashlight?" And he said, "Well, it's in the car." And I said, "Well you might better go and get it." And he said, "What d'you mean?" And I said, "Well, I'd like to see you do like what you done when I wasn't here." And he said, "I would if I want, but I don't have to take your advice." And I said, "All right, you're here for inspection. Okay," I said. "You've got just three minutes," I said. "If you're not out that door in three minutes' time," I said, "I'll throw you out." So he went around, and he must have been out again in two minutes!

Partly it was a generation gap; partly a difference of class and culture. As Jack Bain told me, "Our staff was comprised of experienced cheese men. Not necessarily college graduates or anything. But somebody who'd learned cheese and could go into a plant, talk the cheesemaker's language, and actually make cheese — and supposedly good cheese."

Complaints got back to the Minister of Agriculture, occasionally prompting a memo to be sent to the Dairy Branch, like this one, for example:

This is not the first such criticism that has come from this area, in a round-about way, in the past couple of weeks. Two other dairy operators I know have expressed similar concerns (one at Molesworth, one at Goderich). The gist of the complaint is that our inspector in the area is not only brusque and a bit on the officious side, but he seems intent on making demands of these local dairies that are simply beyond their abilities to provide. The impression is very evident in that part of the province that this ministry intends to impose such stringent regulations on the operators of the small dairy plants that they will eventually have to close down and resort to central processing. This they greatly fear, and I think with a great deal of justification.[7]

By 1956, the worst of the offenders had gone out of business. Of the 410 Ontario cheddar cheese factories that closed between 1941 and 1956, 82 per cent were small factories making less than 75 tons of cheese a year and were often the worst offenders in terms of sloppy production methods.[8] Three-quarters of them were in Eastern Ontario.

Other problems remained, including the multiplicity of voices, often with contradictory priorities and concerns. For instance, large, capital-intensive and increasingly automated dairy plants making a range of dairy products such as yogurt and cottage cheese as well as pasteurized cheddar cheese wanted a guaranteed supply of milk to keep their facilities running at full capacity. As well, recent immigrants making "specialty cheese" — popular Canadian versions of European classics such as Parmesan, Camembert, and Emmenthal — had little in common with traditional Ontario cheesemakers.

But the main problem was the oldest one: the entrenched poverty of Ontario cheddar after a century of dependency on British cheese importers who controlled the market. Now cheddar vied for space in the domestic market against lower-cost processed and other cheese made by automated machines, while traditional cheddar remained the most labour-intensive of

Harrowsmith Cheese Factory in 1955 (above) and later in the 1980s (below) after construction of the new plant.

all dairy products and therefore irreducibly costly compared with mass-produced machine-made cheese.[9]

The Department of Agriculture recorded the decline passively, in the calm bureaucratese of its annual reports.

1956: "A considerable amount of mechanical defects occurred in cheese at a few factories where the makers refused to accept the instructions given by the board fieldmen. . . . Many of the older factories are now closing, having allowed their plant and equipment to depreciate to a state where it was unprofitable to repair or replace. New and larger and better-equipped plants are taking their place." It also noted the shortage of skilled cheesemakers and that "lucrative" wages as labourers on the Seaway were luring men away.

1959: ". . . a shortage of skilled cheddar cheese makers" — though European immigrants are bringing knowledge of other cheeses and cheese-making methods.

1960: "The smaller plant is experiencing difficulty in competing under present day conditions. . . . Shortage of skilled makers. . . . Fifteen plants making 'fancy' cheese. . . . Four plants burned."

1961: "Plants manufacturing milk products have continued to show improvement in equipment and construction. . . Shortage of cheesemakers for cheddar. . . . Two factories burned."

1962: "Two factories burned."

1963: "Two factories burned."[10]

George McLaughlin's Marketing Board

The collapse of the British cheese market was only one blow, although certainly the most symbolic. Ontario cheddar was also pummelled internally, by a number of sources. One was the sudden blizzard of exacting government regulations, with the onerous cost of compliance. Another was touched off as farmers turned from cheese factories to other local markets wherever they could get a few more dollars for their milk. But now, cheddar's legacy as the poor cousin of the dairy industry and convenient dumping ground for surplus milk rebounded. The standard of low prices set by cheddar dragged down other prices, frustrating other farmers who were trying to get better returns on their milk by organizing into their own producer groups and trying to control supply.

Because the fluid-milk market was the most lucrative, it was also the most competitive and most fraught with power struggles. In the mid-1930s, there were some 1,600 milk distributors across the province — most of them selling unpasteurized milk.[1] They overlapped delivery routes. They stole each other's customers. And they played farmers off against each other to get milk cheaper if they could. It was chaos.

The Ontario Whole Milk Producers' Association, formed in 1925, lobbied the government for some regulatory order. In 1934, the government created the Milk Control Board, which licensed distributors and began organizing them into set delivery areas, with specified farmers as milk suppliers. Pasteurization was encouraged and, in 1938, it was made compulsory.

Slowly, marketing and pricing agreements were worked out — although in 1958, prices for fluid milk ranged from $6.12 a hundredweight in Northern Ontario to $3.40 in Glengarry County.[2] But the worst problem was the lack of control over who could be designated a "fluid" milk producer. Cheese factory patrons jumped at almost any offer that improved on the pitiful returns for cheddar cheese, especially after the collapse of the British market in 1952. The Milk Producers' Coordinating Board was set up in 1954 to try to resolve these problems by creating a single plan for marketing all farmers' milk in the province. The board had representatives from all four of the major milk producers' groups: fluid, butter, cheese, and concentrated milk.

These weren't delegates from the elected farmers' groups such as the Cheese Producers, however; they were appointed by order-in-council. (Ev Biggs described this later as "a subtle move.")[3] This created another organization to speak for Ontario dairy farmers and designated it "the official contact between the Milk Industry Board and producers."[4] Yet its representatives were potentially more beholden to the government appointing them than to the farmer groups for which they were ostensibly speaking.

The corporations associated with the Ontario Dairy Processors' Council wanted their council to be made the industry's official representative to government. But they had to content themselves with having their representatives appointed to the government's reactivated Industry Advisory Committee.

Mike Simpson represented the powerful Ontario Milk Distributors Association, and Sam Ault of the Dairy Council represented the processors: everything from condensed milk and ice cream to cheddar cheese, plus brick, Colby, and the new "specialty" cheeses derived from Europe.

Sam Ault's roots were in the cheddar business. His father Jack had started with a single cheese factory at Cass Bridge, near Winchester in Eastern Ontario, then expanded into managing a string of factories in the area, forwarding supplies and hauling the cheeses to the weekly cheese boards. He also produced special milk products for Ogilvie Flour and signed a contract to make cheese in bulk for Kraft. When Jack died, Sam's brother, Ken, sold his half of the business to Ogilvie Flour. Sam himself stayed on, though he was less interested in cheese and other milk products than in the business end of things.

"I got interested when it started to expand," he told me later. He expanded into condensed milk and whey-powder. He also expanded his cheesemaking for Kraft, using funds from the Cheese Factory Improvement Program until it stopped in 1965. He had written a thesis on cheese factory consolidation when he was a student at the Ontario Agricultural College. Called "The Role of Consolidation and Factory Expansion in Reducing Cheese Manufacturing Costs," the thesis was based on research into the first cheese factory amalgamations under the Cheese Factory Improvement Act in the early 1940s. Ault graduated from the OAC in 1947, one year after George McLaughlin and one year before Ev Biggs.

A factory in Brockville represented "the first big expansion in Ontario," Ault recalled, "and that's what really got me going, because I said, 'If we can do it there, we can do it all over Ontario.' And we did it." In his next project, he amalgamated three factories to build one large new one at Wolfville. In a third project, he amalgamated some of his father's old factories to build a new plant at Winchester.

Ault involved himself in the political as well as the business end of the dairy industry, informally by joining the fishing camp frequented by the top executives of the big dairy companies — "I think our associations with Kraft were made a lot in fishing," he said later. More formally, he joined all the industry associations going: the Ontario Cheese Manufacturers'

Association, the Ontario Dairy Products Manufacturers Association, and the Milk Powder Manufacturers' Association. As these were amalgamated into the Ontario Dairy Processors Council (later, simply the Ontario Dairy Council), he became head of the cheese division, then the concentrated-milk division. In the late 1960s, he was elected vice-president and finally president of the Dairy Council.

"Somebody had to do it, to take some leadership, and I could see that by devoting my time I was going to make my own business better," Ault commented. "And also, all kinds of regulations were being put in, so we had to have a strong association to make sure that the regulations that were put in were the correct regulations."

In 1960, the Milk Industry Act was amended to allow for the creation of a unified provincial milk marketing board, and a provisional one was set up. It would tell the government what it wanted and needed, and the government would deal with the industry through the Milk Control Board and the industry advisory committee. Understandably, the strongest groups representing the most powerful interests set the tone and the priorities. A formula price for fluid milk was agreed upon first, with other prices to be negotiated somewhere below that amount. That was the hard part, especially with Hector Arnold resisting the fluid milk interests every step along the way.

Sam Ault's original plant, 1933 (above), and after considerable expansion, 1984 (below).

Sam Ault (left) attending a Cheese Festival Dinner as Chairman of the National Dairy Council.

It is impossible to know Arnold's motives. Maybe he was trying to buy time for the cheese producers until improved markets gave them a better bargaining position with other interests in the dairy business. Maybe he was simply pig-headed and stupid, refusing to see the writing on the wall. The message was clear to all the others, including, it seems, the vice-chairman of the Cheese Producers', Bob Kelso.

Attending government meetings in 1961, when Hector Arnold was apparently sick,[5] Kelso agreed to a plan whereby the provisional milk marketing board would begin pricing all farmers' milk in Ontario. When Hector Arnold resumed his duties, he was soon at loggerheads with the chairman of the government-appointed producers' board, Emerson Farnsworth, a fluid milk producer. Farnsworth complained that the cheese producers were making an integrated milk marketing plan unworkable.[6]

Farnsworth approached Jim Baker, who had replaced Ev Biggs as Dairy Commissioner when Biggs became deputy minister. Baker then met with Bill Stewart and suggested that things be moved along with an inquiry. To this, as Jim Baker recalled years later, Bill Stewart said, "Gosh, we can't do anything about an inquiry. We'll have to get a request in from the producers."

Curiously, the cheese producers' representative was not present at the November 5 meeting which called for such an inquiry. When the vote came down to a tie, Emerson Farnsworth cast the deciding vote in favour of this intervention.

By spring 1962, the inquiry was in place, chaired by University of Toronto economics professor S.G. Hennessey. There were two other commissioners: Frank Wood, treasurer of Abitibi, and Jack McArthur of the Royal Bank. Ev Biggs described them as "foils for his impatience and stubbornness. Hennessey was a hard taskmaster."[7]

He had taken on a big job: nothing less than laying the groundwork for comprehensive (and soon, national) supply management in the dairy industry. This included at least a little discrediting of certain approaches, certain organizations, and certain individuals along the way. Hennessey's report passed sweeping judgment on the management practices of both Ontario dairy farms and farmer-run dairy organizations:

While farmers increasingly are regarding their occupation as a business rather than a way of life, there still appears to be a considerable lack of understanding of basic economic principles, and a continuing failure to adopt a business-like approach to the farm operation. Many don't understand the difference between current and capital expenditure. They have no real understanding of depreciation or returns to land, capital, labour and management.[8]

It was expected that the Hennessey Report would devote the largest space to discussing the fluid or whole-milk producers. In fact, a lot of people understood that the whole inquiry was largely intended for that group, a perception borne out by the preponderance of briefs coming from whole-milk producer groups or from associations such as milk distributors in related businesses. Furthermore, the first initiatives recommended by the inquiry, and subsequently implemented, responded exclusively to fluid milk producers. This worked to the detriment of other milk producers by tacitly ranking them as less important.

One of the surprises of the report was the space it devoted to the Cheese Producers' Marketing Board. Through a series of embarrassing excerpts from minutes of board meetings and other internal business, the report did a character assassination on the Cheese Producers' Association and its chairman, Hector Arnold. It insinuated that Arnold was secretly working for the British buyers, and certainly not in the best interests of cheese factory patrons.[9] It also suggested that he'd engaged in some underhanded dealings, for instance, to expand the producers' warehousing facilities through a suspicious purchase at Oxford Station and substantial changes in the building plans.[10]

"Hennessey really had it in for Hector," Jim Baker told me later. In fact the original text was so harsh that Baker requested that it be checked by a lawyer. Its release was delayed while some of what Baker had worried was "libellous material" was edited out. What remained was damaging enough.

Having noted that 10 British firms accounted for 91 per cent of the imports of Ontario cheddar, with one firm accounting for 27 per cent of the business, Hennessey concluded that "there is limited competition between British cheese importers."[11] He found it "very strange" that one year Hector Arnold had refused to sell cheese to some new British buyers who were even willing to pay two cents a pound more than the traditional buyers. (According to his widow Ina, Arnold had feared alienating his friends, the traditional English buyers, who sent Ina and Hector a Christmas card every year.)

Years later, Arnold Johnston, Secretary to the Cheese Producers' Marketing Board, recalled that Hennessey took him aside one day during the inquiry and asked him outright if Hector Arnold was getting money under the table from the favoured British importers. Johnson was flabbergasted that his boss was thought to be that powerful. But he shook his head, no, he didn't think so.

In other matters, the report noted that Mr. Arnold had been chairman of the Cheese Producers' Marketing Board for nine consecutive years, and that he'd drawn a per diem every single working day during 1963.[12] In a long aside dealing with the Cheese Producers' warehouse facilities, it noted that an extension to the board's cheese-storage warehouse in Belleville had gone ahead without a call for tenders or consultation with the board. It went into detail over a discrepancy in the amount of money the Cheese Producers were said to have paid to buy additional storage facilities at Oxford Station. It also noted that some of the land proved to belong to the CPR, yet no title search appears to have been made to discover this before the purchase was closed.[13] The minutes of a special board meeting 17 August 1964, and a subsequent one held September 14, were reproduced in full as Appendices I and II in the final Hennessey Report. They read like a travesty of due process as Hector Arnold strove to cover up his actions and the poor judgment they betrayed. The August 17 minutes record that the following resolutions were passed:

1) That the directors of the Ontario Cheese Producers' Marketing Board accept the search of title of Oxford Station property made by Mr. H.C. Arnold and Mr. A.E. Hicks.
2) That the directors of the Ontario Cheese Producers' Marketing Board are satisfied with the policy on the export price of cheese being used at the present time in 1964 by H.C. Arnold and J.A. Johnston, and have no criticism to offer.
3) That we the Ontario Cheese Producers' Marketing Board, [assembled] here in

Belleville on August 17, 1964, have investigated all the records and minutes of all Board meetings where reference has been made to the building of an addition to the Belleville warehouse. We find by the minutes there was approval by the board on the following:

a) that nothing had been done without the full knowledge and consent of the whole board. . . . And finally, the board finds everything in order and assumes full responsibility in connection with the building of this warehouse as it now is one of the best, up-to-date and modern cheese warehouses in the Province of Ontario and possibly the Dominion of Canada — Carried.[14]

The report of the Ontario Milk Industry Inquiry recommended among other things that the authority of the existing board of the Ontario Cheese Producers' Association be suspended.

Thirty years later, Hector Arnold was still being cast as the villain of the piece. In the opening pages of his book on the OMMB, Everett Biggs described the Cheese Producers' under Hector Arnold as "a virtual one-man show. . . . Arnold was one of those who didn't like interference. He'd gotten away with a deceptive show of interest and concern regarding the overall changes that were needed in the milk marketing picture. . . . In reality, however, Arnold was really interested only in cheese, and to all appearances, in retaining his own authority and position."[15]

Who knows? Hector Arnold died before research on this book began. But it's possible that he became a convenient scapegoat for the cumulative neglect of the cheese industry. He was just a small-time operator with a grade-school education and too much ego to know when he wasn't fooling others but was himself being actively conned. Gordon Henry, who negotiated with him on behalf of Canada Packers when that company traded and warehoused a lot of cheese, remembered those occasions fondly:

He was a real backwoods type. You had to josh him and kid along with him. I used to tell him, "You're the judge, the jury, and the hangman. You've got us at your mercy." He'd smile and puff on his pipe (which he mostly left unlit). But, well, I guess a hard-nosed businessman would have done better.

As for the $15 per diem, it appears he indeed collected it for every day he worked, and that he put in many days. He used the money first to install electricity and plumbing in the farmhouse, and later to send his two daughters to college. Ina and a hired hand kept the farm going, milking the 12 to 20 cows, while Arnold dressed up in his suit and horn-rimmed glasses and went to town. He wheeled and dealed the best he knew how in a business world increasingly peopled by academically groomed professionals. He secured the loyalty of board members like A.E. Hicks by sending him on a lobbying trip to Toronto with an overnight stay at the Royal York Hotel, which had little packets of soap you could take home with you.

Within months of receiving Hennessey's Report, Bill Stewart had legislated the creation of the Ontario Milk Marketing Board (OMMB) which could take in, market, and distribute all milk in the province. He had also appointed the members of its inaugural board of directors. He had promised that farmers would have a chance to ratify these initiatives in a referendum, though none was ever held.[16]

Stewart's first choice as chairman of the OMMB was the man he'd first wanted to chair the industry inquiry that had laid the groundwork for it; the man his predecessor (Bill Goodfellow) had sent to England with Ev. Biggs in 1960 to take a look at the English milk marketing board; the ex-president of the Holstein-Friesen Association; the man who Hennessey had quoted repeatedly throughout his report, referring to him as "one of Ontario's foremost milk producers,"[17] and elsewhere as "a prominent farmer."[18] The man was George McLaughlin.

George McLaughlin grew up on a prosperous dairy farm near Oshawa where his great-great uncle Robert had launched the McLaughlin Carriage Works in the 1870s. While one of Robert's sons had joined in the McLaughlin-Buick project, the other carried on with the farm. In turn his son, Ray, became one of the first master Holstein breeders in Canada and among the first to install bulk milk storage and automatic milking machines.[19] To groom his son George to take this over one day, Ray sent him to the Ontario Agriculture College. There, George displayed a range of talent and ambition. He became speaker of the mock parliament and head of the college Parliamentary Club, a member of the College Royal executive (which staged miniature versions of cattle shows such as the Royal Winter Fair), and advertising manager for the college yearbook, the *Libranni*. When he graduated in the class of 1946, he was described in the *Libranni* as "an authority on everything from temperance to Clydesdales." In 1956, George sold the family farm to E.P. Taylor and moved the fluid-milk dairy north of Toronto to Beaverton. Within five years, he had it sufficiently established to impress Professor Hennessey and give him a model against which to judge others as lacking.

McLaughlin had been involved in the policy end of the dairy business for some time, both at the bureaucratic level, from his brief days (after college) as an agricultural representative, and at the political level. As he explained,

I knew Bill Goodfellow, you see, because he and his son showed cattle. He was a cattle breeder, and I remember judging when his son would be showing. I met him a couple of times, got to know him. And the government here sent me over to England — see, I'd been speaking about these problems to farm meetings and milk producers and cattle breeders. And you'd go to the Royal Winter Fair to show cattle, and the only topic of discussion would be what the hell are we goin' to do about this milk business.[20]

McLaughlin was a gifted speaker, with a knack for telling a story and a voice for playing the part:

There isn't anybody else in society that has a contract that some guy can break and you can't do a bloody thing about it. You sign a contract to guarantee to supply them [milk distributors] with so many pounds of milk a day, and then one day he phones ya up and says, well, I don't want it today. And you say, but I got a contract, and he says, well go get a contract with somebody else. So you don't have a contract; he has one. He's got you tied up, but you don't have him tied up. Because he's big and he's a dairy, and you know they're big shots, and you know they'll just go and get some other farmer's milk. In the meantime, you've got $150,000 to $200,000 tied up in the business, and it doesn't make any sense.

The year Hennessey launched his inquiry, George used the occasion of attending an international Holstein meeting in England to renew his contacts with the British Milk Marketing Board and its chair Dick Trehane:

He lined up one day with the director of production, the next with the director of transportation, and their legal people the last day. It was beautiful; a short course in how to run a marketing board. So when I came back, I started relating this experience at some of the meetings I was at. I knew this [Hennessey] group was interviewing people all over the country, and I was trying to hurry up and influence things before they got the report all written up. So I got invited to meetings because people knew I'd been over and I was past president of the Holstein Association, and you get invited to speak at banquets and so on.

One of McLaughlin's first moves as the Milk Marketing Board's powerful chairman was to hire the capable Lorne Hurd away from his post as general manager of the big-business-dominated National Dairy Council to serve as general manager of the Milk Marketing Board. He also raided Dominion Dairies, 80 per cent owned by Kraft, to staff the positions of director of marketing and production.[21]

In its first phase of operations, the OMMB dealt only with fluid milk producers, giving them a Group One quota and marketing what milk they produced within it to licensed dairies and concentrated-milk plants. Under a "graduated entry" policy, as other farmers installed bulk tanks and met the qualifications to become fluid producers, they too were given Group One quotas. Eventually, the board had more milk on its hands than the fluid trade could handle. The Ontario Dairy Council, with Sam Ault as its first chairman, recommended an auction for the surplus milk. This was rejected, as Jim Baker recalled, for fear it would favour the big companies over the small ones; however, an alternative plan — namely a classified pricing system — was adopted. The system set different prices for different "classes" of milk — from Class 1 for fluid milk, down through Class 3, for cream, cottage cheese, and yogurt, to Class 5, where milk for cheddar cheese was priced the lowest, but available to cheese factories only when demands by the other milk-industry segments had been satisfied. Brick and Colby cheese plus sterilized milk for export were all to have been in Class 5 as well; however, at the last minute, brick and Colby were moved into the Class 4 price category along with specialty cheese. Being in Class 5, receiving only the "residual" milk in the province's milk pool, would soon have disastrous implications for cheddar as the National Dairy Policy came into effect.

The National Dairy Policy was developed through the late 1960s at the same time the OMMB was fine tuning its own policies and regulations. George McLaughlin was president of the Dairy Farmers of Canada in 1966. This gave him considerable influence in that policy-making process as well as insight into the effects it would have provincially.[22] The key implication was contained in the national market-sharing quota (MSQ), by which each province was allocated a share of milk production across Canada to meet, and not to exceed, domestic needs. Introduced in 1968 and adjusted annually according to national milk-consumption patterns and, in turn, parcelled out among each province's dairy farmers through production quotas, the MSQ set a limit on the amount of milk each farmer could produce. This in turn limited the amount of milk flowing into each province's milk pool. Yet under the OMMB's pricing system, all the companies buying milk from the OMMB everywhere from the bottled trade, ice cream, and yogurt through to brick, Colby, and specialty cheese received as much milk as they needed. Cheddar, the traditional "balance wheel" and dumping ground of the dairy industry, was dependent on whatever milk was left. Each cheese factory was assigned a "plant supply quota" for sharing this residual milk.

Taken as a whole, the National Dairy Policy was a brilliant adaptation of the National Policy from manufacturing to agriculture and, within it, to the cheese industry. It directed farmers and, through them, cheese producers away from the vagaries of international competitiveness and even the option of selling in the export market. Instead, it adjusted their production to fit the needs of the domestic market only and penalized surpluses.

By 1970, the policy was in place, and the OMMB had completed its takeover of all milk, all milk marketing, and all milk distribution in the province.[23] For farmers at the receiving end of OMMB's administration of provincial and national policy, it was akin to becoming part of a state-run General Motors. If they hadn't become shareholders or executive officers, they at least were lifetime employees with their quota as their badge of seniority.

The cheese business was reoriented to fit the miniature replica model associated with branch-plant manufacturing. No longer specializing in cheddar, a quality product like Swiss chocolate and Swedish furniture which can compete in world markets because of their reputation for excellence and craftmanship, the cheese industry was redirected to produce Canadian versions of French Camembert, Swiss Emmenthal, Greek feta, and Danish blue, plus cheddar. Between 1965 and 1970, production of these "Class 4" items tripled to 13,340 tonnes. At the same time, cheddar cheese production dropped by 13 per cent as milk supplies for cheddar cheese making began to diminish.[24]

Then the export market began to pick up.

Shutting Down Hector Arnold

Supply management was unfolding as planned. Bureaucrats representing big government and big business were building a national system for integrated milk production, marketing, and distribution. It was centrally controlled and, increasingly, monitored by computers.

There remained, however, one stubborn anomaly: the Ontario Cheese Producers' Marketing Board and its still-active former chairman, Hector Arnold. The legislation creating the Ontario Milk Marketing Board had made all other milk producers' organizations redundant. The trick was how to effect this redundancy with the least political fuss — in other words, how to "bell the cat," as Jim Baker recounts the language used by one government insider. The cat was Hector Arnold. So a meeting was held, and a deal was struck. Hector would become a special consultant on cheese marketing to the OMMB, receiving a modest retainer. In return, Hector would cooperate with a proposal to merge the Cheese Producers' with the OMMB, with the latter taking over the cheese exchange at Belleville.

"It was all very hush-hush," Lorne Hurd of the OMMB recalled later. "And it worked like a charm." [1]

Stage one was for George McLaughlin and George McCague (Milk Commissioner responsible for OMMB policy) to speak to the January 1966 meeting of the Cheese Producers' Marketing Board in the place of the scheduled speaker, Jim Baker. They outlined the benefits of joint milk marketing and the appropriateness of producer organizations like the Cheese Producers' amalgamating with the OMMB. Jim Baker remembers telling the two Georges afterward: "Gosh, the way you fellas handled that, you could sell refrigerators to Eskimos."

After they'd spoken, someone moved a resolution from the floor endorsing the notion that the Ontario Cheese Producers' Marketing Board and all its assets should be absorbed into the OMMB. [2] Bob Kelso, in the chair, moved discussion along to a vote, which passed.

Stage two occurred a month or so later when the board's lawyer had prepared the necessary papers transferring the cheese board's assets (including all the warehouses) to the OMMB. With these in hand, he accompanied George McLaughlin and Jim Baker to the first meeting of the new board of directors in Belleville.

"It was all done very smoothly, and it was over in 15 minutes," Jim told me later.

When they arrived, unexpectedly it seems, Hector Arnold had to explain why they were there. George McLaughlin stressed that this was a follow-up to the resolution passed at the annual general meeting in January, and the lawyer put the papers on the table.

George Wood, cheesemaker at Ivanhoe, was one of the new board members present. "I'll never forget the day they come down to that meeting and they said, 'that's it; the Cheese Producers' is no more.' That was the part that hurt. They just said, 'that's it.' " [3]

Looking back on it, Jim Baker thinks the board members never had a chance. "They didn't really know what they should do; what questions they could ask. They were befuddled by it all."

Someone asked, what do we do? The lawyer said, sign here. They did, and that was that. Nearly 30 years later, Jim Baker still feels a little guilty about it all, especially about Hector Arnold, whose services as a consultant were never used. This seemed to confirm the widely held view that Hector Arnold had been bought off, pure and simple. It apparently hurt Hector Arnold very much and continued to wound his widow, who held Jim Baker personally responsible for the matter.

"It was a buy-out all right," Jim Baker admitted. "But I had intended for Hector to be a real adviser. It always bothered me that he wasn't made use of."

His disappearance left only two men representing cheese-milk producers on the milk marketing board — two voices out of 14, on a board dominated by its "tough and aggressive" chairman,[4] one of whose favourite retorts was apparently: "You may be right, but I don't agree with you."[5]

The Closing-Out Program

They kept at it.

In Perth County, Fred Day branched out into specialty cheese, though he still made cheddar, and passed on his knowledge to his son-in-law Harold Douglas when Harold took over as cheesemaker at the Blanshard and Nissouri plant at St. Mary's, turning out traditional raw-milk cheddar for the English and other overseas markets. In East-Central Ontario, Harold Kingston brought his son Bruce into the business and talked about diversifying into new and different types of cheese as a way to survive. At Plum Hollow, Claude Flood still made his daily batch of culture and used a fist full of curd to see if the whey was ready to run. At Warkworth, Doug Rowe and his son Bob kept making cheese for Kraft, though when tourists stopped by, on pilgrimages for their children to know their roots, they took a moment to show them through the "make" room. Like John Fraser and a few others, Doug Rowe got an old butcher's display case and started selling a bit of cheese directly "over the counter" as well.

The bulk of cheese production was now concentrated in the Eastern counties, where the soil was good for little more than pasture. Here too, small family farms meant large seasonal swings in milk production, which small, seasonally operated cheese factories were in the best position to accommodate. Many of these were still farmer-owned cooperatives, including La Co-operative Laitiere de Lefaivre and the St. Albert Cooperative in Stormont County. Many still closed during the winter, when milk supplies dwindled; however, this was becoming more difficult with increasing capital costs — not just for making cheese but for disposing of whey and complying with government health regulations. All round, it was getting harder and harder to carry on.

Yet it seemed no one in government would take the cheddar cheese business seriously, on its own terms. Industry people on the Dairy Council wanted to solve the cheese factories' problems by closing them all down and letting the big multi-product companies take over everything. Agriculture Minister Bill Stewart decided that another inquiry was in order. In

Fred Day displaying his specialty cheese (left hand) and traditional cheddar (right) in the storage room of his Atwood Cheese Factory.

May 1968, he asked Jack Bain, head of Milk Products with the Dairy Branch, to lead it. It was Bain's last best chance, and he gave it all he could in the six months he had before retirement.

The terms of reference asked him to investigate "the problems facing the industry" and "the feasibility of establishing alternative facilities necessary to provide producers with the best possible returns for their milk." Whatever agenda was implied in this directive, Jack used the inquiry as a chance to rebut the big-is-beautiful rhetoric associated with the Hennessey Inquiry, with Department of Agriculture economists, and the Ontario Milk Marketing Board; and to defend the cheddar cheese industry on the terms to which he'd devoted a lifetime's work and passion: as a traditional handcraft accountable to values other than the purely technical ones of efficiency and productivity.

He began his report with some comments on efficiency which, he said, had been stressed as almost the paramount priority in numerous submissions to his inquiry. He then asserted that "efficiency in the context of this report refers to the costs of producing a high-quality cheese."[1] Having qualified "efficiency" as subordinate to the larger social or cultural goal of "high-quality" cheddar, he went on to cite figures showing that this product was still selling at "a substantial premium" in Britain and the United States. Drawing on his own and others' experience as craftsmen, he then argued that a very large plant using automated equipment to process pasteurized milk into cheese cannot possibly produce the same quality of aged cheddar as the smaller plants which are still run on hand craftsmanship, using raw or heat-treated milk. To sustain the tradition of Ontario cheddar, Bain said it was essential to support medium-sized cheddar-cheese factories and even some smaller ones in tourist areas.[2]

In six months, Bain assembled an impressive defence of Ontario cheddar. Having made his case that it was essential to let small and medium-sized factories make traditional raw-milk or heat-treated Ontario cheddar because the process required the total control and involvement of an experienced cheesemaker, Bain marshalled statistics that showed a steadily rising demand for cheddar in Canada and some recovery of the export market since the disastrous post-war period. He even conducted a supermarket sales study, which showed a consistent preference for aged cheddar over mild or medium. By contrast, per-capita consumption of processed cheese, while indisputably greater than the demand for cheddar, had actually declined between 1966 and 1967.[3]

He also challenged efficiency on economists' own ground by citing a 1956 departmental study which showed that medium-sized factories enjoyed the lowest unit production costs, with the very large factories registering higher costs and the smallest factories having the

Bright Cheese and Butter Manufacturing Company Ltd., 1987, Bright, Ontario, where specialty cheese accounts for 95% of production, cheddar only 5%.

highest. The author of this study had actually downplayed this finding, virtually dismissing the lower costs as deriving somewhat speciously from "unpaid family labour" and not including "depreciation costs." Yet many of the very large plants had "management" as well as labour costs and were often unable to operate at full capacity.[4] (Large plants complained that the smaller cheese factories prevented them from running at full capacity and undercut them in price.)

Jack Bain recommended support for a pluralistic cheese industry. He argued that the medium-sized factories (such as Warkworth, Balderson's, Harrowsmith), which were producing four times the volume they were in 1950,[5] largely through amalgamations under the Cheese Factory Improvement Program, were eminently suited to supply quality cheddar to the export market and some segments of the domestic market. The very large multi-product plants were best suited to make processed cheese and mild pasteurized cheddar, plus brick, Colby, and specialty products for the domestic market. And a few small factories, such as the Forfar Dairy in Leeds County, should be left as they were. A steady trickle of people dropping by for cheese and a chat showed that there was a place for these, as living icons of Ontario heritage.

Above all, he warned, "a sudden demise of cheese factories" would destroy "the economic base of many small communities." Furthermore, he added, the government had a "moral obligation" arising from the just-ended Cheese Factory Improvement Program under which, he said, "many factories did amalgamate and spent considerable funds to stay in business."

Therefore, he concluded:

— Amalgamation of existing factories should be restricted.
— Substantial additional investment in highly automated cheesemaking equipment . . . is not warranted at this time.
— The formation of additional multi-purpose plants in the province of Ontario is unnecessary at the present time. . . .[6]

Jack Bain knew his report was bucking conventional wisdom bordering on gospel truth. He was right. His recommendations were seen as "totally unacceptable." As Jim Baker put it, "the Bain study was set up with the idea of what to do about the cheese factories. And he didn't recommend anything. He wanted to leave everything the way it was."

By then, Jack Bain had retired and couldn't defend his vision within the government's bureaucracy. He was powerless, therefore, when the Ontario Milk Commission (successor to the Milk Industry Board) set up another inquiry, co-chaired by Murray Stewart of Dominion Dairies and Bill Murchie, one of its own vice-chairmen and a produce merchant known as "a good Conservative."[7]

A year later, this inquiry submitted a report completely contradicting Jack Bain's analysis. "In broad terms, the industrial milk processing industry in Ontario is characterized by too many plants, undercapitalized and with little faith or optimistic outlook for the future. . ."[8] It went on to say that there were some 45 cheese factories whose "return on investment is unsatisfactory by any standard, [and which] often charge no depreciation on their operating statement." These factories shouldn't be in business, the inquiry asserted. Therefore, it concluded, the government "should encourage plant consolidations, in the interests of eliminating the inefficient plants which this study found are seriously affecting modernization and efficiency of processing milk in the province."[9] Further, it recommended that this should take the form of partially forgiveable loans to "efficient milk plants" for use in "buying out and closing down inefficient plants" with the clear understanding that they could never reopen.

Within a year, the Ontario cabinet had approved a "Plant Consolidation Assistance Program." It was open to creameries and milk-powder plants, but was principally intended for cheese factories. It would eliminate half the remaining cheese factories in Ontario. It was scheduled to cease in August 1973 but was extended to December. By this time, cheese fac-tories were getting only 50 per cent of their original quota of milk, and there seemed no end in sight to the steady shutting off of supplies. Barry Haggett, a farmer on the board of the Plum Hollow Cheese Factory, remembered many phone calls from the Milk Commission, which was administering the program. "We were contacted again to say, we've extended it. They almost harassed us with reminders."[10]

Yet the market for Ontario cheddar had been improving. In Canada, consumption of cheddar cheese reached a new high of 162 million pounds in 1971, compared with 156 million in 1970. As well, the British cheese market had revived, with vigorous sales through 1970 and 1971, and at prices sometimes 33 per cent above Australian and New Zealand cheese. But the Canadian dairy policy, once in place, was rigidly biased towards satisfying domestic requirements only and resisted changing course for what it considered to be an unpredictable international market. Nothing was done, either federally or provincially, to increase milk supplies flowing to cheddar cheese factories to accommodate this demand.[11]

In the end, 43 factories were closed under the program, 33 of them cheese factories and 10 concentrated milk plants.

Equally to the point was where the factories' milk-supply quota had gone, now that dwindling milk supplies were beginning to make the quota virtually a franchise to make cheese and the key to surviving in the national milk-management system. Four companies received 66.3 per cent of the quota transferred under the consolidation program. These were Kraft, Ault's, Cow and Gate (which Ault bought out a short time later), and Gay Lea, a remnant of the United Dairy and Poultry Cooperative established by the United Farmers of Ontario in the 1920s.[12]

Sam Ault took a certain pride in having helped launch the "closing out" program, as cheesemakers called it: "I'd gone to college with the deputy minister [Ev Biggs], so I took the idea to him first, and it was compatible with the government's own idea, 'why don't you get large, more efficient factories?' "

He had every right to be heard. In 1969, he was past-president of the Ontario Dairy Council and vice-president of the National Dairy Council. As well, Ault and Murray Stewart, co-chair of the Murchie-Stewart Inquiry, both indirectly worked for Kraft, which gave them considerable common ground.

Sam Ault didn't care whether the program paid the large plants to buy out the smaller ones or paid the smaller ones to sell out to the larger ones. His major concern was with the plant-supply quota attached to the plants to be sold out:

We decided a long time ago that we were gonna buy all the quota we could buy; even though the plants often weren't large enough to handle them. We had to throw out whey or things like this for years, 'til we got the plants large enough to handle them. But we owned the quotas; that was the main thing. And once we got the quotas, then expansion just seemed to fall into place, because customers had to come to us.

In the end, Ault's would control nearly all the milk for cheesemaking in the province of Ontario. In the end, too, Ault's was bought out by Labatt's, which in turn was bought out by Brascan, a giant multinational corporation.

I grew up ignorant of all this because what we learned at school was Ontario's military and industrial history, nothing about rural institutions and ordinary people. On the television I watched in a Montreal suburb, the programs all took me away, into Mickey Mouse on Fridays, Zorro on Saturdays, and *Walt Disney Presents* on Sunday. As well, while my father tried to create some continuity for us in the Ontario countryside, we were only weekend farmers. "Hobby farmers" was the term locals used, and not politely, to describe people like us who came out from the cities, bought up derelict farms, and hired help to pretty them up.

Because we worked the land ourselves, planted trees by hand, and helped restore the fields to a semblance of fertility, I thought we were exempted from the derisive label. But now I wonder. We never really set down roots. We didn't have the time to commit ourselves fully. We subscribed to the weekly *Glengarry News* but never cultivated the rural routine of reading the "Births," "Marriages," and "Deaths" columns every week to follow the doings in the neighbourhood. There was the occasional piece of local poetry, rhyming couplets about things like the sunset behind the Mill Pond. I found them corny and sentimental.

The farm was a superficial connection, just weekends and summer holidays. And as snow filled the quarter-mile laneway in late November, we suspended our subscription to the *Glengarry News* and packed it in for the season. For six months at a time, we didn't know what was going on. We didn't hear when John Fraser sold his last cheese factory to Ault's; didn't even notice when the Graham Creamery stopped making cheese and focused solely on butter.

While the cheese factories were there, we took them for granted. And when they weren't, we never wondered why.

The Kraft Boycott

My generation came of age sensing that something was missing. We sensed that the unfolding technological universe, with its principles of profits and productivity, control and dependency, was a spiritual wasteland. We couldn't articulate this at the time. We could only go on instinct. Instinct drove us to reject the establishment world view brought to us by big business via the "idiot box." We did this by dropping out and protesting everything related to American imperialism, from corporate domination of the Canadian economy and culture to military oppression in Vietnam.

In 1967, opinion polls revealed a sharp reversal from long-standing public indifference to foreign investment in Canada. Sixty-seven per cent of Canadians thought the government should take steps to reduce foreign control in Canadian industry.[1] In 1971, the New Democratic Party (NDP) under David Lewis launched a major attack not only against foreign ownership of the Canadian economy but on Big Business as a whole. That year, Lewis published *Louder Voices: The Corporate Welfare Bums*, arguing that the Canadian Government served big business more than the citizens as a whole, and that the biggest beneficiaries of the welfare state weren't citizens but large, often American-controlled, corporations thriving on grants and "forgiveable" loans.

By the mid-1960s, non-Canadians controlled 60 per cent of Canada's manufacturing sector, 74 per cent of the petroleum and natural gas industry, and 59 per cent of mining and smelting.[2] In terms of industry concentration, by 1972, the 100 largest U.S.A. manufacturing companies controlled 48 percent of all assets. The highest concentration was in metal manufacturing, followed by food, chemicals, and petroleum refining. American branch plants in Canada were dominant in all of them.

In the dairy industry, Kraft was merely the largest of the giants, with sales of $161 million in 1971, followed by Beatrice Foods with $135 million, Silverwoods with $118 million, and the Cooperative Agricole de Granby with $82 million.[3] Kraft controlled an estimated 50 to 80 per cent of the cheese market in Canada.[4] Also, with its 80 per cent control of Dominion Dairies, Kraft was a power in the fluid milk and related businesses. Dominion Dairies and Borden were found to have acquired 63 per cent of the 2,000 independent Canadian dairies that were bought out between 1922 and 1963. By 1961, the three largest dairies —Silverwoods, Borden, and Dominion Dairies — controlled roughly 40 per cent of the milk, cream, and buttermilk market in Canada and around 60 per cent of the market in the 17 largest cities in Ontario. As early as 1959, a Royal Commission on Price Spreads had found that five firms controlled 87 per cent of the processed cheese market in Canada, with Kraft being by far the market leader.[5]

Kraft came to symbolize American imperialism, partly because it was so ubiquitous, both in media advertising and in everyday life. Its product line had become so central to the lives of most consumers that it was almost impossible to get through a day without at least one Kraft product: Kraft dinners and salad dressings, Kraft's Parkay margarine, Kraft peanut butter, jams, jellies, and marmalades, Kraft barbecue sauce, Kraft caramels and toffees. Whether it was Velveeta, Cheese Whiz, or Cracker Barrel cheese, Kraft was *the* name in cheese, especially in Central Canada, where it marketed 75 per cent of Ault's cheese production and virtually all the cheese produced by the Cooperative Agricole de Granby, which accounted for 60 per cent of Quebec's entire cheese production.

But Kraft cheese, especially plastic-wrapped cheese slices, also stroked a deeper pulse of revolt. Kraft and its "plastic cheese" represented the triumph of the big, the bland, and the artificial over the local, the particular, and the authentic. Kraft and its cheese thus came to epitomize the soulless technological dynamo of modernity.[6]

When it began, however, the protest that came to be remembered as the Kraft Boycott wasn't directed against Kraft. The villain had no face as yet, unless it was the computer at the Ontario Milk Marketing Board's head office in Toronto. The protest first emerged as an outpouring of rural rage over the changes being imposed on farmers by the government, not just in Ontario but across Canada. The changes were pushing aside the small family farm with its mix of a few hens, a few pigs, and dozen or so cows in favour of fewer, larger farms specializing in a single line of agribusiness.

On the federal side, the government wanted to get out of subsidizing exports, having paid $54 million in export subsidies on cheese, butter, milk powder, and other exportable dairy products in 1964 and $172 million in 1968. It introduced a "subsidy eligibility quota" for dairy farmers in 1968, imposing a limit on the amount of milk used for cheese and butter making on which it would pay an export subsidy.[7] A year later, it restricted payment of this subsidy to only those farmers whose industrial milk production exceeded 12,000 pounds. Since the subsidy amounted to roughly a third of farmers' milk income, the effect of the restriction devastated smaller producers.

At the same time, the Ontario Milk Marketing Board was having its own rationalizing effect through its standards that, for instance, required farmers to meet to qualify for Group 1 quota. When the OMMB introduced its market-sharing quota plan for industrial milk in 1970, the federal government dovetailed in a set of levies or deductions from farmers' milk payments — first to recover the costs of exporting surpluses and second to penalize farmers for producing more milk than was their share of the province's portion of national production requirements.[8] Yet throughout this period, dairy farmers were still not making much money.

Between 1966 and 1971, the number of dairy farmers in Ontario dropped by 40 per cent. Twenty thousand simply went out of business. At the same time, the proportion of farms with 12 cows or fewer declined from representing half to representing only a third of the whole, the number of farms with more than 32 cows nearly doubled, and the number with more than 93 tripled.

Barry Haggett, a farmer from Plum Hollow, was on the OMMB's county milk committee at the time and can remember farmers' frustration:

There were many people got into trouble with their quota because, well, you had to gear your production to 8 per cent in August and 13 per cent in September, and you were penalized if you didn't meet this monthly quota. But there were many couldn't figure it all. They wouldn't realize they were running out of quota, so they'd be charged for overproduction.

And it wasn't just this. They were changing policy not by the year, but by the month. They were putting levies on and taking levies off, and they were putting subsidies on sometimes, and they'd never had a subsidy on before. And the whole thing was a mumbo-jumbo.

In theory, Haggett was on the milk committee to represent farmers' concerns to the OMMB and to tell the OMMB what policies were relevant:

But you weren't long finding out that you weren't there for that. If you really wanted to help your neighbour, and he was being forced out, you'd be told: well, this is board policy, and they'll have to conform to board policy. When they set a deadline for the end of cans, that was it! It was all for the good of the dairy industry, not for the individual. They didn't care about the individual farmer, it seemed, just the dairy industry. And I don't think there was one of them lost any sleep over it. But I know a lot of farmers who did.

Farmers found themselves with no outlet for their over-quota milk. Once they exceeded their quota, the OMMB stopped picking up their milk, but the OMMB was the sole marketing agent for milk in the province. Farmers couldn't just deliver it to the local cheese factory, yet at Plum Hollow, Claude Flood was desperate to take it, because the English market had picked up considerably in the past year, while milk allocations through the plant-supply quota had dwindled. Cheese factories had originally been guaranteed 98 per cent of the amount of the "base" quota they were allotted in 1968. By 1971, however, they were getting only 62 per cent of their base. The situation was driving factories into the arms of the closing-out program, forcing them to embrace at least a cushioned defeat.

One day, some farmers took their milk to the factory at Plum Hollow anyway. The OMMB refused to authorize a sale to the farmer-owned cooperative, so Claude Flood couldn't by law receive it. Frustrated, a couple of farmers dumped their milk onto the road outside the factory. Word spread. Other farmers came and dumped their milk down the hill too. Then someone phoned the media.

"The milk was running down the road high, wide and handsome. It was in the hot weather, so it created quite a stink," Barry Haggett recalled. "It wasn't fun, but it wasn't solemn neither. People were saying things like, I can't see how they can do this, how can it be legal, how can it be tolerated? . . . Wasn't there supposed to be a referendum on all this?" Yes, but none was ever held.

In July 1971, the Chairman of the Plum Hollow Cheese Cooperative wrote to Agriculture Minister Bill Stewart following a meeting at the community hall, which had been filled to overflowing. There, he reported, local farmers had passed a resolution calling for George McLaughlin's removal as Chairman of the OMMB. He ended, saying: "We do not intend to surrender easily to a man such as George McLaughlin who is bringing strangulation to the Ontario dairy industry and who is allowed to run at large by the Ontario Government."[9]

It wasn't the only such letter. The Deputy Minister of Agriculture recalled: "We were kept busy drafting replies to letters from people who wanted to get McLaughlin fired."[10]

By then, George McLaughlin had been chairman of the OMMB for six years, though his initial appointment had been for only two. The press in Eastern Ontario described him as "that banty rooster from Toronto."[11]

There were two ways of describing the problems, depending on your point of view. From a rural perspective, the problem was of once-independent farmers, craftsmen-cheesemakers, and local cheese factories betrayed by a remote and uncaring complex of big government and big business. The second, more urban point of view, focused on big business and, specifically, big multinational American business gaining control of the Canadian economy. The National Farmers' Union took up the cause in terms of the first interpretation. Students associated with the New Left and the Waffle wing of the NDP focused more on American big business. They didn't always intersect.

Through the late 1960s, the Farmers' Union had been staging tractor demonstrations to publicize farmers' continuing low incomes and apparent forced march into agribusiness. Their predominantly young leaders were accustomed to seizing the initiative. So it wasn't preposterous

when someone suggested that the Ontario Farmers' Union should become a bargaining agent for Ontario dairy farmers and negotiate directly with the big dairies to get farmers a better deal for their milk than the OMMB was providing.

Former student radical Fred Gudmundson from Saskatchewan was the NFU's Director of Organization and Education — or, "organization and agitation" as he called it. He joined Walter Miller, NFU farmer-director for Ontario, in an ad hoc round of phone calls to the dairy companies with a view to meeting to discuss direct negotiations.[12] Sam Ault at Winchester was friendly and agreeable. Come on in, he said. Later, he was to tease his friend Russ Greenwood, President of Kraft Foods, that he should have done likewise: invited them in, given them a cup of coffee, listened to what they had to say, thanked them for coming, said goodbye, and gone on to other business. But when the phone call came to Mr. Greenwood's Montreal office and his secretary asked who was calling, Greenwood refused to take the call. He later explained, quite reasonably, that what the NFU wanted to discuss was improper: the OMMB was the farmers' designated sales representative and, as long as this was so, he had no business negotiating with the Farmers' Union.

Gudmundson had just returned from a farmers' tractor protest in Prince Edward Island where, he said, the police had virtually chased him off the island. Now he was ready for action in Ontario. One of the vanguard of young leaders to emerge from the 1960s youth movement, Gudmundson was active in the NDP Waffle, which had formed in 1969 as a radical left wing of the NDP, dedicated both to liberating Canada from American corporate capitalism and transforming it into a grass-roots democratic socialist society. In 1970, Gudmundson was among those backing the young Don Mitchell as a candidate at the Saskatchewan NDP leadership convention where Alan Blakeney was confirmed as leader. At the time, Mitchell was doing postgraduate work on multinational agribusiness at the University of Regina. He happily shared what he'd discovered with his friends.

What was needed was a venue for publicizing this information. Then someone suggested demonstrating for higher milk prices for farmers at a Kraft facility, the big cheese factory at Ingleside, near Cornwall. Farmers had staged a protest outside one of the big Borden plants some years before, when Borden supposedly imported cheap milk powder from Ireland, depressing the local market.

Gudmundson phoned the NFU office in Saskatoon, where staff member Don Kossick had a network of contacts from his days with the Canadian University Press. John Deverell was working for the Ontario Agriculture Department and knew some of the Toronto media. Don Mitchell pulled some notes together

on the multinational proportions of Kraft. A microphone and loud speaker were rented. A press release was prepared, run off, and distributed to the press. And at eight o'clock in the morning on 28 July, 1971, the demonstration that was to launch the Kraft boycott began.

Standing on the back of a pickup truck, Fred Gudmundson addressed a crowd of what the NFU later estimated to be 1,000 angry farmers. The *Ottawa Citizen* later reported that "what the NFU wants — naively, it seems — is for the processors to reduce their profit margins and pay more to the milk producers."[13]

Gudmundson listed the dimensions of the cost-price squeeze in which farmers found themselves because the OMMB wouldn't keep price increases in line with the rising costs of complying with all the regulations it imposed on them for participating in its milk pools. Speaking next, the gravel-voiced Walter Miller said that farmers could dump their milk, except they only hurt themselves that way. Why not withhold their milk in the same way as city workers withhold their labour in a strike?

When the marketing board trucks began arriving at 9 a.m. with loads of milk for the huge multi-product factory the Ontario government had given Kraft half a million dollars to help build, the farmers set up a picket line.[14] The truckers turned aside, parked in a vacant lot across the street, and sat there eating sandwiches and milk thoughtfully provided by the protesters. Police and protesters remained at a standoff until noon, when the marketing board redirected the trucks to Ault's big plant in Winchester and to the Carnation plant in Alexandria.[15] The next day, the OMMB announced a substantial increase ($1.15 a hundredweight of milk) in industrial milk prices. The NFU issued a press release claiming victory. The OMMB countered that the increase had been in the works long before the NFU took their action and suggested that the NFU might even have staged their demonstration simply to exploit the anticipated announcement.

The matter might have ended right there had it not been for one piece of rhetoric that surfaced in the sweaty exercise in participatory democracy that July day at Ingleside: the rhetoric of "boycott." It isn't known who first suggested the idea. What mattered more, at least as Fred Gudmundson recalled it later, was that the word had "a certain ring to it." It was a Canadian version of the California grape boycott.

Students returning to university campuses in the fall cleared Kraft products out of campus cafeterias and joined NFU picket lines outside large supermarkets where they helped distribute bright-coloured leaflets about the globe-bestriding proportions of Kraftco. There were teach-ins at universities in Toronto and Ottawa, as well as in Winnipeg, Regina, and Saskatoon, with speakers from the Committee for an Independent Canada, the NDP Waffle, and the NFU. There were meetings with store managers, union groups, women's groups, and consumer groups. There were bumper stickers, buttons, and posters. There was a *Kraft Boycott Supplement* to the NFU's monthly newspaper, containing expressions of solidarity and support from such labour leaders as Terry Meagher (Ontario Federation of Labour), Homer Stevens (United Fishermen and Allied Workers), Harry Munroe (Winnipeg and District Labour Council), and Ross Hale (Saskatchewan Federation of Labour.) A hundred thousand copies were distributed.

Working through the student movement, Don Kossick spearheaded a special publication by the Canadian University Press called *The Great Food Tabloid*, the contributor list for which reads like a partial "who's who" of the emerging New Left in Canadian Politics: Cy Gonick, John Deverell, Don Mitchell, John Warnock, Warren Carragata, Mary Jane Elgar, and Dorothy Wigmore, among others. Its articles include "Food Pollution," "Advertising and Workers' Wages", "It's Mainly Because of the Deceit," "Agribusiness Octopus," and "Shutting Down Dairy Farming in Ontario." Over 10,000 copies of this special edition were distributed to student groups, abortion-rights and other women's groups, consumer groups, and ad hoc Kraft boycott and grape boycott information centres across the country. As well, the Gestetner in the back room at the NFU office churned out countless single-sheet boycott flyers, featuring recipes for alternatives to most, if not all, of Kraft's products or listing alternative brands to the ones made by Kraft.

The boycott grabbed the attention of the big-city media. In September, the *Toronto Star* ran an editorial questioning the closing-out program as a sell-out to the big American dairies: "Canadian taxpayers are subsidizing the American companies that are forcing Canadian dairies to close down and put people out of work. Something has gone very wrong with the Ontario Milk Marketing Board." At the OMMB, George McLaughlin wrote a letter to the editor vehemently setting the newspaper straight.[16]

The burly and garrulous NFU president, Roy Atkinson, appeared on national television with Caesar Chavez, the leader of the Farmworkers of America and of the famous California grape boycott. Jim Laxer and NDP Waffle colleague Don Mitchell appeared on Peter Gzowski's popular new radio show *This Country in the Morning*.

The media didn't probe much below the surface rhetoric. Nor did reporters go into the country to talk to the last of the old-time cheesemakers in the last of the craft-scale cheese factories at Forfar, Harrowsmith, Plum Hollow, Warkworth, and the like to discover why they weren't all behind the boycott too.

When Doug Rowe heard that the NFU was trying to get cheese factories exempted from quota restrictions on the milk they could receive, he wanted to do all he could to help. But when this meant joining a boycott against Kraft, he couldn't back up fast enough for fear his contract with Kraft would be broken: "There was no company done as much for the dairy industry as Kraft. I mean, they do the advertising for the entire dairy industry in Canada. We're beholden to Kraft." Indeed.

The fate of Jean Chamberland's Cremerie Plantagenet in Eastern Ontario's Prescott County provided a lesson in case any was needed. Jean Chamberland grew up above his father's garage business in Plantagenet and started working at 15. After the war, he started his own factory, expanding it in the 1950s under the Cheese Factory Improvement Program.[17] When his new plant opened in 1958, he also followed the local trend and signed a contract to make cheese for Kraft. It worked out fine until 1970, when the OMMB classified milk for brick and Colby at a higher price than milk for cheddar cheese. Kraft abruptly cut its contract with Plantagenet and moved its brick and Colby business across the border into Quebec where milk was cheaper.

Chamberland would have been gone under then and there, for the Kraft contract accounted for 90 per cent of his business. But he pleaded with Albert Ouellette, Kraft's country buyer, whom Chamberland had always regarded as "a gentleman." They worked out a deal. Chamberland would make brick and Colby, but he'd be paid less for it; as well, he agreed to lend his plant-supply quota of milk for cheddar cheese to

Kraft, which used it to keep the Ingleside plant operating at full capacity until it could install the equipment it needed to make a more diversified range of cheese products. This continued until September 1973, when Kraft abruptly cut off orders for Chamberland's cheese. Having just invested in new cheesemaking equipment, Chamberland was left with little choice. He sold out the business to Ault's. Ault used the Plant Consolidation Program (due to expire that month, but then extended until December) to subsidize the purchase.

No one covering the Kraft Boycott asked why these cheesemakers were so dependent on Kraft and why neither the provincial politicians nor the government bureaucracy were willing to champion their concerns.

What Price Heritage?

Ontario cheddar had ceased to be a presence in the dairy business. The industry was virtually monopolized by multi-product plants, the corporate conglomerates that owned them, and the industry associations that represented their priorities to the government — directly through lobbying and indirectly by moving in the same social circles. Out in the countryside, meanwhile, traditional cheddar cheesemaking was down to 20 or so small and medium-sized factories — a mix of farmer-owned cooperatives and private affairs owned by cheesemakers. Outsiders in their own province, they were being starved out of existence for lack of milk.

Through the 1970s, their base quota had dropped to 56 per cent, then to 50 per cent, then 46 per cent of what they'd been guaranteed at the beginning of the market-sharing quota system for industrial milk. Ontario also lost 8 per cent of its share of national milk production.[1]

It didn't matter so much to the big dairy companies making a variety of milk products in the miniature replica model of Canadian manufacturing. As supplies of milk for cheddar cheese declined, they increased their milk orders for brick, Colby, and other products. Of course this left even less for the craft-scale cheddar cheese factories. Between 1968 and 1974, the production of brick, Colby, and other kinds of cheese increased 96 per cent. Cheddar production dropped by 22 per cent. Some cheese factories were running at 40 per cent of capacity — hardly a paying economic activity.

At Warkworth, Doug Rowe had bought out another local plant solely for its milk quota, just to keep going. He was selling more cheese "over the counter" now and had to pay more for this milk — considerably more than what the Board charged for specialty cheeses and nearly what it charged for brick and Colby. Yet the Board had refused all appeals to have that milk exempted from the plant-supply quota. Now he was close to retirement, with two sons to consider. Bob wanted to carry on and groom his own son, then 14 and helping out at the factory, to take over when he, in turn, retired. But the eldest son, John, favoured selling.

Ault's had been dangling offers for a while. Doug worried, however, that if Ault's kept buying all the other local plants for their supply quota, and if the plant-supply quota were cut back again, the Rowes might have no choice but to accept whatever price Ault's was willing to give them, or close for lack of milk.

Across the way at Harrowsmith, Bob's hockey buddy Bruce Kingston felt the same way about the cheese business: he wanted to keep at it. So the two young men decided to get active in the Ontario Dairy Council. They drove to Toronto to meet with the Dairy Council's cheese committee, chaired by Keith Henry of Ault's. They hoped to get the Dairy Council, of which they were members, to go to bat for them. Instead, they got the runaround. They were told they should diversify into specialty, brick, and Colby, for which they could get unlimited supplies of milk to keep their factories running at full capacity.

In fact, they had both considered this move

Top: Eldorado Cheese Limited, near Madoc, Ontario, famous for "Gold" brand cheddar.

Bottom: Empire Cheese & Butter Co-Op, near Campbellford, Ontario, the only cheese factory left in Northumberland County, shown here in 1930.

but preferred to stick to what they knew. As Bob Rowe put it, he'd heard that the specialty market was "a cut-throat business. But cheddar's kind of an old honour system. You know, a handshake was a commitment, and no one would ever consider going back on an agreement, for a year at a time anyway. Oh, and there was pride too, sure. Cheddar, that's all I've known and my dad and his dad and mother before him."[2]

Also, the British were back in the market, paying top price for traditional Ontario cheddar. "That was the frustrating part. Why do we have to do this, get into specialty cheese, when we know we have the cheddar market out there?"

In the summer of 1978, a consortium of English buyers came to Canada with an order for 1.5 million pounds of aged Ontario cheddar. But the little cheese factories weren't able to fill this extra order unless the plant-supply quotas were relaxed and more milk let into the system. The OMMB refused to do this, agreeing with advice from the Ontario Dairy Council that, since the English market wasn't reliable, this might leave a costly surplus of industrial milk in subsequent years. It offered instead to bring cheese across the border from Quebec, which the Ontario factories could age and package to fill their regular orders. The Ontario cheesemakers stubbornly refused.[3] As Bob Rowe put it:

Other provinces, like Quebec, are taking up the slack, but we could have been filling that market if we could have had the milk. And what was Canada famous for? Cheddar cheese. They say Canadian cheddar, but it was Ontario cheddar they wanted. So our feeling was, why should they jeopardize the cheddar for the specialty? Why jeopardize the backbone just to let this other one grow? Not that you shouldn't keep the specialty cheese; I don't mean that.

Sometimes, the cheese committee agreed that there was a problem; but to solve it, they said, the federal government must increase Ontario's share of Canada's total milk production. (This had been parcelled out at a time when Ontario's milk production was in a slump and Quebec's was booming.) The federal people would say it was a provincial-allocation problem and leave it at that.

Time and again, Bob or Bruce asked that cheddar cheese be removed from the residual milk class. They would be told: "But that would leave the butter-powder people to carry the whole brunt of it; it would wipe them out." They would suggest exempting the craft-scale factories from the quota and be told: " 'But you can't discriminate between a small factory and a large factory if they're both making the same kind of product."

"Hell," Bruce said, "they'd have more reasons than Carter has pills."[4]

Once, when they got back to the car after a meeting, Bruce just sat there banging his forehead against the steering wheel. Driving home to Hastings County, Bob would try to be reasonable:

You can't imagine the specialty cheese guys wanting to change the system where they can just phone up and order the milk, you know, whenever they want it, and year round, and all just for paying three cents a pound more for the milk, while these guys at the bottom are taking the brunt of everything. If they could see our point or not, they'd never admit to it anyway. The way the system was set up, why should they?

Back in Warkworth, Bob dropped by at the neat, whitewashed cheese factory where his father was "just finishing up," as the older man would say. He'd tell him the latest from Toronto, and Doug would tell him if one of Ault's people had come by.

Then they got word that the marketing board was considering a further cut to cheese factories' quota: this time, down to 42 per cent of their base quota. Bob Rowe talked to Bruce Kingston, and they agreed: "What have we got to lose? Let's throw a little bit of money into the pot and form our own association and see what we can do about it." They split up the

Logo for the Pine River Cheese & Butter Co-Operative, Ripley, Ontario.

Wilton Cheese Factory, Wilton, Ontario, 1993.

names of the people associated with the 20 or so craft-scale cheddar cheese factories that were still in operation and invited them to a meeting. Seventeen men and women turned out. From Western Ontario, old Wes Krotz sent his son Ken, and Glen Martin sent his son Donald from Pine River. Lawrence Lalonde came from Balderson Cheese. Don Sills came from the Mapledale Cheese Factory north of Belleville. Talmage Stone came representing the farmer-run Forfar Dairy, and Claude Flood came from Plum Hollow.

Talmage Stone was nearly 80 years old but still in fighting trim. Long-time dairy farmer and reeve of the local township, he had fought to keep the local railway station, school, and post office. He'd been associated with lost causes since, at 13, he drove the family buggy taking neighbours to the polling station to vote for Wilfrid Laurier and free trade in 1911. "I've always been rebelling against anything that would take away our identity," he told me later. "And the cheese industry, why this is the identity of rural Ontario — Eastern Ontario anyway. I grew up in it."

The meeting ended with the formal creation of the Ontario Cheddar Cheese Association, resolved to go over the heads of the Dairy Council board of directors and even the Milk Marketing Board. It would appeal directly to the Ontario Milk Commissioner for either an exemption from the plant-supply quotas for cheddar cheese factories, a freeze on quotas, or a change in the classification system to put brick, Colby, and specialty cheese into the residual class, on the same beggar's footing as cheddar cheese.

Bob Rowe was chosen president of the association and Bruce Kingston its secretary-treasurer. Together, they prepared their case, in the form of a five-page brief, typed neatly with narrow, economical margins. It began with a polite caveat: "We would like to emphasize at this point that we are in no way trying to undermine the Ontario Dairy Council . . . and we look forward to a long alliance with them." It then went straight to the point: "The number one problem in the Industrial Milk field is the severe shortage of Market Sharing Quota, for the province of Ontario." It explained the history of this problem, referring to some market research which indicated an escalating demand for quality Ontario cheddar both within Canada and abroad. (The research was part of a larger study commissioned by the Ontario Milk Marketing Board in 1973, which had been ignored.) It laid out the Association's suggestions for getting more milk into cheddar cheese production. And it evoked the debt of history: "We must now ask ourselves, 'Are we going to let this great industry wither and die, or are we finally going to take the steps to preserve an industry that is as much of our Ontario Heritage as farming itself?' "

They presented the brief to the Ontario Milk Commission in April 1978 and waited for the response. They were immediately criticized by the Ontario Dairy Council, which was probably to be expected. What they hadn't anticipated was the virtual silence from the Milk Commission. The most it agreed to do was to look into the matter, which the Dairy Council had been doing for years.

Maybe it was time to give up, to either adjust to the status quo and diversify into specialty, brick, and Colby, or sell out to one of the larger companies better adapted to modern dairying as a commercial business, not a creative craft integral to a rural community. But Talmage Stone wouldn't let them give up. He'd learned perseverance from decades walking behind his team of workhorses pulling the single-furrow "walking plow," as it was called. It took 10 days to plow a single field and he'd done it every fall. Maybe, too, this fifth-generation Loyalist was just a bit stubborn. As well, he had no faith in government bureaucrats. But he did have faith in people: the hundreds of ordinary people who brought their children and their grandchildren out to the country to places like Forfar to see a genuine hand craftsman at work and to buy a wedge of traditional Ontario cheddar. Why not let them know the plight of Ontario Cheddar, he said, by getting up a petition?

The petition was printed in simple black letters on 8-by-11-inch sheets of yellow cardboard. It said:

HELP!!!
Due to policies beyond our control
the cheddar cheese industry
of Ontario is being threatened
by extinction
If you enjoy Ontario Cheddar Cheese
And would like to see a
Continuing supply available
Please Sign Below

"Below" was a 39-cent school scribbler, left open on the cheese counter. Posters and scribblers were placed in every one of the little craft-scale cheese factories during the summer of 1978. Most by then had permanent counter facilities and sold local handicrafts as well as cheese. But it was the cheese that drew in the customers. When they read the petition, they signed in droves.

As the signature count topped the 30,000 mark, members of the Ontario Cheddar Cheese Association felt their point was made. They also had a lawyer who felt there were grounds to challenge the Milk Marketing Board's authority and was prepared to do so all the way to the Supreme Court of Canada.

Representatives of the Marketing Board, however, told the Toronto press that the Cheddar Cheese Association was being melodramatic and suggested that the cheesemakers it represented were simply unwilling to face reality. Privately, officials from the Marketing Board warned Rowe and Kingston that contesting the board's authority could turn into years of costly litigation.

Later, Doug Rowe said with a nervous hearty laugh: "I often wonder. I wouldn't want this to get back to Ault's or anything, but I sometimes wonder along the way if there wasn't something said between the Marketing Board and Ault's, sort of 'Get that fella out of business.'" Another hearty laugh. "Like I said, I wouldn't want this to get back to Ault's, but I sometimes wonder. . . ." Because suddenly, there were more calls and visits from the people at Ault's:

When it all boiled down, we just didn't know there was anything down the road 10 years from now. Like I said, we figured, we're down to 49 per cent of our quota now; if this keeps going and we get down to 25 per cent, we're not even gonna have enough milk for to supply our own stores, let alone to sell to Kraft's. We could get right down to where we'd have nothing to sell, and we'd just have to turn the key. So we figured, "Well, we'll put a price on it."

Ault's made the Rowe's an offer they couldn't refuse. Not only did they promise a job for each of the sons, they'd even pay Doug a retainer to run a small store-front operation at his plant in Warkworth, taking in Ault cheese made at its largely automated plant in Winchester and packaging it under the old Warkworth label. Ault's would also look after every one of the Rowe's staff and even maintain its commitment to the local hockey team.

"They're very public-relations conscious." Bob had to give them that. But still he was torn:

I hated to give up the fight of the whole thing. But I had to look at my family's whole stake in it. . . . My brother, it wasn't the personal problem as it was to me; I guess I'd taken it as my own pet thing, not to say that the others wouldn't have done the same thing. . . . But how far does a person go? Do you jeopardize a sale that would set your own family up and look after all your employees? But then I'd think, well all those other people are still there, and they're going to keep this thing going. And if they don't, well, whose fault is it? Their own. If it was just going because of me, well, how good was it anyway?

On the last day of 1978, they made the last batch of cheese at Warkworth. When they finished, they scrubbed out the vats as usual. They washed and hung up the shovels. They swept and hosed down the floor and hung up the brooms on their appointed hooks. And they threw out the last few bits of curd. Eventually, there was nothing left but the sound of Doug's grandson crying: "I think that's what hurt the worst. Because he figured maybe he'd be working here too and maybe carrying on. He'd be more or less the fourth generation in it."

Over at Harrowsmith, the Kingstons got a partially forgiveable loan from the provincial government to help them build a new semi-automated cheese factory to produce Mozzarella and Parmesan as well as brick, Colby and cheddar cheese. They signed a contract to make it all for Kraft. Bruce Kingston began drifting back to Ontario Dairy Council meetings, where in a couple of years he was elected to the board of directors. But by then he no longer considered himself a cheddar cheesemaker. "I guess I'm more a specialty cheese manufacturer now. It used to be you just put your head down and made cheese, but now it's more of a business. You got to worry about advertising and inventories and per-capita consumption."

Afterword

Cheese Factory replica, erected 1964,
Upper Canada Village

In the end, Harrowsmith was bought out by McCain Foods of New Brunswick. Ault's was taken over by Labatt's and Labatt's in turn by the Brascan business conglomerate.

In the end, too, it became virtually impossible to sustain the traditions of Ontario cheddar in today's technological society.

As I worked on this book, I felt like an archaeologist gathering fragments of old and broken vessels. All I had was faded bits and pieces, but they had an aura about them. There were phrases that spoke of a loving attention to detail: doing a thing well for its own sake, not for making money. There was evidence of caring that suggested fellowship and community and an abiding commitment to those relationships. These values were not unique to rural Ontario but were rooted in medieval craftsmanship. Most of that culture died out under the twin forces of commercialism and industrialization in the modern era. But vestiges survived in the margins, away from the cultural mainstream.

A century ago, the poet and artist William Morris launched what has been called "the greatest design revolution of the 19th century" to reverse the degradation of creativity he sensed occurring in the mainstream of English society. He traced this degradation to the new philosophy of commercialism, which reduced all life to commodities and private property, and which was shaping industrialization in the 1870s and 1880s. He switched careers from writing poetry to reviving medievel craft techniques and technologies in the manufacture of quality wallpaper, wall hangings, carpets, furniture, glassware, and ceramics — not just for the rich but for everyone. He sold these from his store on Oxford Street in London to a fleetingly eager clientele across England and abroad, including Canada, in an effort to prove that creative involvement was the pillar of a healthy society and that people would return to it if given a chance. In lectures and essays, Morris spelled out his vision for an "earthly paradise," achievable by restoring creativity, and an appreciation of it, in daily life and labour.

"Art," he said, "is man's expression of his joy in labour" — that is, in creative involvement in work and life in general. Furthermore, he argued, it is meant to be imbedded in daily life, not set to the side on a pedestal. In societies predating the separation of art from everyday life, he noted that even the most "intellectual" of art was meant to engage and please the bodily senses and that even the simplest of crafted products "shared in the meaning and emotion of the intellectual. One melted into the other by scarce perceptible gradations; in short, the best artist was a workman still, the humblest workman was an artist."[1]

At that time, too, he said, "the unit of labour was an intelligent man. Under this system of handiwork, no great pressure of speed was put on a man's work, but he was allowed to carry it through leisurely and thoughtfully; it used the whole of a man for the production of a piece of goods, and not small portions of many men; it developed the workman's whole intelligence according to his capacity."

Morris described the elements of craft creativity as including fellowship and continuity of tradition; doing a thing "duly" — that is, as an end in itself, not primarily for making money; self-respect deriving from a sense of usefulness in society; variety and the hope of creating something fine and possibly even unique; and an almost sensuous pleasure in "the deft exercise of bodily powers."

These essays provided me with a frame in which to place many of the stories in this book: Claude Flood devoutly making his daily batch of starter cultures and, from a lifetime's craftsmanship, having only one vat's worth of cheese judged less than the highest grade; Harold Kingston and his quirky personal techniques for testing the curd or for isolating the source of impurities coming in with the morning's milk; Fred Day battling his board of directors to give him the tools he needed to do his job well and fussing to get the seam straight on the cheese he was finishing for exhibition at the British Empire Show. And rallying around them all, big Jack Bain like some latter-day William Morris trying to defend the cause of craftsmanship in a sea of big government and big business, with their built-in biases toward commercial, industrial technology and prescriptive, regulatory bureaucracy.

Where Morris's words went beyond the individual exercise of craftsmanship to include the broader social context of fellowship and community, I thought of the informal leadership good cheesemakers gained in the community and the farmers bound together by their shares in cheese-factory cooperatives. I recalled a visit to the Forfar Dairy on a spring evening in 1982 when Talmage Stone called an emergency meeting of the board of directors because one of the 17 farmer shareholders had passed away.

Talmage was president of the little cooperative, and at 84 years of age, still favoured lace-up black boots, suspenders on his trousers, and elasticized steel bands above the elbow of his shirt sleeves to keep the cuffs clean. He had fought to save the little cheese factory at least twice before. He hated to lose it now because one of its shareholders had willed his share to someone who might treat it as only a commercial investment and sell it to the highest bidder.

For Stone, the Forfar Dairy wasn't a strictly commercial proposition. True, its seven-year-old cheddar, made the traditional craft way with raw — not pasteurized — milk, sold by the ton over the counter and by mail order across Canada, the United States, England, and even as far away as Hong Kong. But that wasn't what kept the factory in business. "It's 90 per cent community spirit, this plant," the old man told me fiercely.

Employing seven people year round and 15 during the summer for tourists, the dairy was the economic hub of the community and, along with Baker's Feed Mill across the street, about the only business left around.

He arrived early for the meeting, anxious to start it right on time. But by 8 o'clock the only others present were the chartered accountant from Smith Falls, Talmage's middle-aged son Ross — also on the board — and his daughter-in-law Marion. Besides being secretary-treasurer for the dairy, Marion Stone ran the local Homemakers' Service, which the dairy helped support financially, organized socials at the community centre, did the bookkeeping, helped Ross run the family farm, and still found time for her own personal craft: hand painting plates.

She busied herself making coffee while the farmer-directors straggled in. Most had come straight from barn chores after a day's spring seeding. Wearing work boots and coveralls, they sat on the old cheese boxes Talmage and Marion had set out behind the cheese counter, their freshly scrubbed hands hanging quiet between their knees.

"Got that big field back of McNabb's in yet?"

"Yup."

After a silence. "Puttin' in oats back there?"

"Mostly corn. Figure the soil's good enough."

Darkness thickened outside. A whippoorwill whistled once, twice, and then fell silent.

Shortly after 9 o'clock, Talmage Stone cleared his throat, and the meeting began. After the minutes of the previous meeting were approved, and some other bit of business taken care of, Talmage turned to the accountant, who launched into a careful exposition of the directors' options vis-à-vis the disposal of members' shares. "Does this mean that if Mr. X dies and wants to will his share to Mr. Y living in Toronto, we can't do a thing about it?" old Mr. Stone asked when he was through. The accountant nodded.

"As far as I know it, yes."

"Then we haven't got controlling interest," Stone countered sharply.

He proposed passing a resolution giving the cooperative the power to buy back shares of deceased members. There was a slight shifting of shoulders and clearing of throats and an almost imperceptible turning to Ross Stone. Rounder of face and softer of mien than his father, Ross Stone gently pointed out that the deceased director might have willed the share to his widow who was still living and active in the community.

"Now, are you going to tell Mrs. Chant that she can't have that share? Are you going to tell her that? What if she wants it?"

Talmage Stone looked hard at his son. He blinked and expelled a reluctant breath. "All right," he said and shut his mouth hard.

Sterling Patterson, another of the younger

farmer-directors, though middle-aged like Ross himself, spoke up reassuringly. After all, he said, the will hadn't even been read yet. Stone looked across at the square-jawed younger man, meeting his eye and offering the makings of a smile. The mood in the room relaxed. Marion Stone laid aside her notebook, slid open the glass door of the cheese counter next to her, took out a wedge of nicely aged cheddar, and carried it into the back where the coffee urn had finished perking.

Following her cue, the directors started gathering themselves to get up. But Talmage wasn't done.

"Are we going to let this whole thing float?" he asked. The directors settled back onto their seats and were silent. Testily, Stone continued: "Well, this means I can do whatever I want with my share, and you can't do anything about it. And the whole company could go down the drain, one share at a time."

Silence. Then Sterling Patterson chuckled softly and looked at the button-nosed Stone: "That's a gamble we'll just have to face," he said. Slowly, more through the presence than the words of these his neighbours, Talmage Stone was reassured. When the will was read a week later, the gamble had paid off. The director had left his share to the cooperative to be dissolved back into the whole. He'd understood.

A decade later, the sense of community was still strong. The craftsmanship in the factory, however, had been curtailed by health regulations, the technologies associated with them, and the burdensome costs involved. It is something William Morris could never have predicted, although, in an indirect way, it all follows from Morris's original concerns about commercialism shaping industrial mass production and consumption.

Forfar stopped making traditional, raw-milk cheddar cheese in 1988, under the pressure of new health regulations and the costs of complying with them. And under the same pressure, the last factory making the original craft product — the Blanshard and Nissouri of St. Mary's, Ontario — went out of business in 1991.

It began in June 1988, when a Health Protection Branch (Health and Welfare Canada) test came back positive for listeria monocytogenes bacteria in some Colby cheese produced at the Blanshard & Nissouri factory, and a testing blitz of all factories handling raw milk was begun.

In fact, listeria exists throughout the natural environment and "can be found almost everywhere," according to a fact sheet on the pathogen prepared by the Department of Food Science at the University of Guelph. Newly improved techniques in culturing bacteria can detect the most minute traces of the pathogen. There's some debate over what levels of contamination pose a real health threat — "what levels really affect people," a grading and inspection representative, Harold MacKenzie told me — and

Blanshard & Nissouri Cheese & Butter Co. Ltd.,
near St. Mary's, Ontario, was the last factory where
traditional, raw-milk cheddar cheese was made before
being forced out of business in 1991.

whether the average person should be the standard, or population groups in the most precarious health: the very old, the sick, and the very young. While healthy adults would only get sick to their stomachs, "high-risk" populations, including newborns, pregnant women, and people with a disease affecting their immune system, risk death — at mortality rates of 20-35 per cent.[2] Pregnant women risk miscarriage. In the interests of universal public health, standards are set "to ensure that no one gets sick," Mr. MacKenzie said.

The Colby test results prompted Health and Welfare to issue a public-health alert, and to widen the testing net at Blanshard and Nissouri to include all its cheese, dating back to 1987. It also prompted an in-depth plant inspection by a dairy-plant specialist from the Ontario Ministry of Agriculture and Food, a Health Protection Branch representative, and one from Agriculture Canada. Following their report, the plant was ordered to shut down, pending modifications to improve overall factory sanitary practices. Blanshard & Nissouri cheese, dating back 12 months, was banned from being sold until tests showed it was clear of listeria contamination.

Meanwhile, the length of precautionary holding continued to be debated while food scientists at the University of Guelph did tests. They found that listeria could sometimes survive for up to 434 days — in cheese ripened at a low 6° C — and for up to 225 days in cheese ripened at the more traditional 13° C. In the end, however, they discovered that the bacteria died off in the natural aging process associated with traditional aged cheddar cheese.[4] As well, as the director of Health and Welfare Canada's Field Operation wrote to his counterparts in Britain in July, "there have been no confirmed illnesses associated with the consumption of these products."

But food-science officials continued to press for the pasteurization of all milk for cheese. This was partly because salmonella bacteria had been detected in some Blanshard and Nissouri cheese in April, and Ministry of Agriculture and Food officials weren't able to trace it back to its originating source in an area farm or farms where they could stamp it out. Investigating scientists, including Don Irvin, Professor Emeritus in Food Science at the University of Guelph who'd done a major study of salmonella in the early 1980s, were adamant: to be on the safe side, all cheese milk should be pasteurized.

The 100-year-old cooperative was stuck. If they pasteurized the milk before making it into cheddar, "then it wouldn't be cheddar cheese anymore," Jack Richardson, then-president of the farmer-owned cooperative pointed out. It wouldn't have the sharp, full-bodied flavour of traditional raw-milk cheddar. In regaining the right to make cheese, they'd lose the right to make their own cheese, the old way. Then Britain's own regulations were changed, banning

Ingersoll Museums, site of the Cheese Factory Museum, dedicated to preserving our heritage.

cheese imports cased in wax. There was also discussion of banning all unpasteurized cheese. The farmers gave up; in 1991, the factory formally went out of business.

In a way, that closure marks the end of Ontario Cheddar as a craft. Nevertheless, a handful of craft-scale factories have carried on, making heat-treated cheese instead of the traditional raw-mild cheddar. But even there, it's a struggle.

At the Forfar Dairy in Leeds County, they've spent $100,000 since 1988 in capital equipment geared to meeting the exacting regulation which have been imposed for making this cheddar — and in proving that they've done so. The investments include $6,800 to install three recording pins on the upgraded heat-treating equipment used for making heat-treated cheese. Two record alternative "set points" for heating the milk (161.5° F., or 72° C. for pasteurized, or 145° F., or 68° C. These records are made every day, then filed for future scrutiny by inspectors. Besides the expense of purchasing this machinery and the cost of tending it, there is a more problematic human effect: subtly discrediting the intelligence of the human craftsman, marginalizing it from the process of making cheese.

The history of making cheddar cheese in Ontario thus becomes an account of government regulation intersecting with commercial industrialization as the making of cheese to make money gained precedence over the making of things for their own sake. Entrepreneurs invested in industrial factories as first and foremost commercial enterprises. Management control, plus increased scale and commercial cost considerations, steadily marginalized the craft principle of doing a thing well. As it did, regulations and safeguards had to be introduced to ensure that things were made well enough. Public health standards grew out of this need first to augment and then to replace the responsibilities which had originally been exercised by craftsmen and their guilds.

Today, these regulations have achieved an almost mindless technological tyranny, which both undermines the integrity of craftmanship and makes it effectively redundant. As Howard French, plant manager at Forfar, put it, "It's all geared to the big plants where they expect people to be robots and not to people who can use common sense. People can no longer think for themselves."[5] The technology does the thinking for them, then imposes that thinking. This meter-reading, meter-heeding, prescriptive approach becomes the dominant culture, turning craftsmen into machine tenders, whether they like it or not.

It is the culture of our technological society, and it not only transforms "them" making cheese. It equally affects "us" eating the cheese as "consumers." It's a continuous, mutually reinforcing loop, as William Morris was prescient enough to notice. In trying to revive the public's taste for quality craftsmanship in turn-of-the-century England, he felt it was essential to replace a superficial involvement in numerous mass-produced consumer goods with a fuller and more creative involvement in living. It was the theme of his utopian novel, *News from Nowhere*, and ran strongly through many essays and lectures.

Elements of his notion of dystopia are visible in contemporary society, where technology does our thinking for us, and even our living. Instead of in-depth experience, in many instances, we consume a simulacrum: a technological chimera. You can see it in what's happened to cheese.

Thirty-five thousand feet in the air flying from Ottawa to Edmonton, I picked up the vacuum-sealed packet of cheese which accompanied the in-flight meal. The label said Kraft Cracker Barrel "old" cheese, cheddar, I assumed. There was a miniature sketch of a horse and wagon on the front — a facsimile of the image presented in television advertisements portraying James Kraft peddling "processed" cheese in the early 1900s. The label also said, "40 per cent less fat," yet fatty acids are essential for aging cheddar and developing the traditional full-bodied flavour. But then, so are bacteria, the free range of bacteria associated with the natural "micro-flora" of raw milk — some of which at least survive in heat-treated cheese. The label

didn't explicitly say "pasteurized" cheese, but it probably was.

I pulled the tab where the arrow indicated and held the package to my nose. A faint smell emerged — a bland, baby-food smell, flaccid as old rubber elastics, not the fecund aroma of traditional aged cheddar. I hesitated, then took a bite. The cheese felt rubbery between my teeth, like curds or very mild cheddar; old cheddar should almost crumble and form a paste in the mouth. I closed my eyes, concentrating on flavour. Yes, there was a bit of a tang. But it was like violins heard through speakers in a crowded elevator.

I put the package down, thinking, that's about all it is: a package of words and symbols from which the original meaning has been eviscerated. Yet all around me, people had swallowed their cheese.

The stewardess interrupted the music coming through my earphones, saying the in-flight movie was about to begin. Could the people by the windows kindly lower their blinds.

I was consuming so many things: classical music on a multi-channel music system, in-flight movie, food, drink, magazines and — until the lowering of window blinds — even landscape. All of it orchestrated by in-flight service schedules. Driven by them, albeit gently and with the friendliest of smiles.

It struck me that this was a slice of life in

technological society. Slightly speeded up and exaggerated, but otherwise typical of normal everyday life. Experience is reduced to a simulation, a series of commodities consumed in a moment.

I closed my eyes, trying to refuse the movie. Trying to recover a sense of myself. I found that I couldn't.

Back home with my son and partner, I break out the packages of cheese I've bought at Forfar. One contains some pre-1988 raw-milk cheese. The other contains heat-treated cheese. A bottle of wine. The evening free. I start with the seven-year old raw-milk cheddar. The flame shoots up the back of my throat, taking me back to Fraser's cheese house and the slow rhythmic cadence of John Fraser's stories. The cheese is rich and multi-hued, with a long afterglow of echoes and variations. The heat-treated cheese is almost as good, except that a veil has been thrown over the raw-milk cheese, muting the flavours a little.

I return to the raw-milk cheddar: a piece of living heritage, now cut off. Soon the last of it will have been eaten, and the memory will fade away.

Unless we choose otherwise, by renewing the craft-like tradition of creative involvement in work and doing the job well. Then we might yet find ways to build on the heritage of Ontario cheddar cheese.

Notes

❦

FOREWORD

[1] Stewart Lane and Glenn Fox, *Synopsis of Economic Research on the Ontario Dairy Industry 1950-1980* (Guelph: School of Agricultural Economics, University of Guelph, 1981), p. 12.

[2] *Report of the Select Committee Appointed by the House of Commons To Obtain Information as to the Agricultural Interests of Canada* (Ottawa: Maclean, Roger & Co., 1884), p. 98.

[3] Earl Haslett, *Factors in the Growth and Decline of the Cheese Industry in Ontario 1864-1924*, PhD. Thesis, University of Toronto, 1969, p. 43.

[4] R.H. Jardine, "The Dairy Branch Serving the Dairy Industry," in *Dairy Branch and 100 Years of Service* (Toronto: Ontario Ministry of Agriculture and Food, 1988), p. 59.

[5] Jack Bain, *Report of the Ontario Cheese Industry Study Committee* (Toronto: Ontario Ministry of Agriculture and Food, 1968).

PART ONE: ORIGINS AND CONTINUITIES

Prologue

[1] Thomas Appleton, *Ravenscrag: The Allan Royal Mail Line* (Toronto: McClelland and Stewart, 1974), p. 81.

[2] Gerald Craig (ed.), *Lord Durham's Report* (Toronto: McClelland and Stewart, 1973), p. 123.

[3] Appleton, p. 54.

[4] Charles J. Humber (ed.), *Allegiance: The Ontario Story* (Mississauga: Heirloom Publishing, 1991), p. 11.

[5] G. Elmore Reaman, *Trail of the Black Walnut* (Toronto: McClelland and Stewart, 1957), p. 128.

[6] C.O. Ermatinger, *The Talbot Regime* (St. Thomas: The Municipal World Ltd., 1904), p. 3.

[7] Reaman, p. 65.

[8] Jane St. Pleasant, "The Iroquois Sustainers," *Northwest Indian Quarterly* (Spring/Summer 1989), p. 33.

[9] Robert L. Jones, *History of Agriculture in Ontario* (Toronto: University of Toronto Press, 1946), p. 6.

[10] Harold Innis, *The Fur Trade: An Introduction to Canadian Economic History* (Toronto: University of Toronto Press, 1970), pp. 26, 31, 36, 143.

[11] Jones, pp. 73, 79.

[12] Leo A. Johnson, *History of the County of Ontario, 1615-1875* (Whitby: Corporation of the County of Ontario, 1973), p. 7.

[13] Mrs. C.P. Traill, *Canadian Emigrant Housekeeper's Guide* (London: Lovell and Gibson, 1862), p. 131.

[14] Susannah Moodie, *Roughing It in the Bush* (Toronto: McClelland and Stewart, 1983), p. 163.

[15] Jones, p. 82.

[16] Royce MacGillivary and Ewan Ross, *A History of Glengarry* (Belleville: Mika Publishing, 1979), p. 293.

[17] William Johnston, *History of the County of Perth* (Stratford: W.M. O'Beirne, 1903), p. 186.

[18] Johnston, pp. 241, 299.

[19] Stewart Wallace, *The Family Compact: A Chronicle of the Rebellion in Upper Canada* (Toronto: Brook & Co., 1922), p. 28.

[20] Robert Gourlay, *Statistical Account of Upper Canada* (Toronto: McClelland and Stewart, 1974), pp. 128, 293.

[21] Thomas McIlwraith, "The Adequacy of Rural Roads in the Era before Railways: An Illustration from Upper Canada," *The Canadian Geographer*, Vol. 14, No. 4 (1970), p. 357.

[22] W.T. Easterbrook, *Farm Credit in Canada* (Toronto: University of Toronto Press, 1938), pp. 25, 37.

[23] Johnston, p. 26.

[24] John McCallum, *Unequal Beginnings: Agriculture and Economic Life in Quebec and Ontario until 1870* (Toronto: University of Toronto Press, 1980), p. 14.

[25] Johnson, p. 99.

[26] D.G. Creighton, "The Economic Background of the Rebellions of 1837," *The Canadian Journal of Economics and Political Science*, Vol. 3, No. 3 (1937), p. 333.

[27] David Earl (ed.), *The Family Compact: Aristocracy or Oligarchy?* (Toronto: Copp Clark, 1967), p. 78.

[28] Douglas McCalla, "The Internal Economy of Upper Canada: New Evidence on Agricultural Marketing before 1850," in J.K. Johnson and B.G. Wilson (eds.), *Historical Essays on Upper Canada: New Perspectives* (Ottawa: Carleton University Press, 1989), p. 246.

Bush Farming, Bees, and Agricultural Societies

[1] McIlwraith, p. 357.

[2] Johnston, p. 33.

[3] Lillian F. Gates, *Land Policies of Upper Canada* (Toronto: University of Toronto Press, 1968), p. 294.

[4] Norman R. Ball, *The Technology of Settlement and Land Clearing in Upper Canada prior to 1840*, PhD. Thesis, University of Toronto, 1979.

[5] Reaman, p. 72.

[6] Jones, pp. 73, 79.

[7] Peter Russell, "Forest into Farmland: Upper Canadian Clearing Rates, 1822-1839," in *Historical Essays on Upper Canada*, p. 139.

[8] H.G. Aitken, "A Note on Capital Formation in Upper Canada," *Canadian Journal of Economics and Political Science*, Vol. 18 (1952), p. 526.

[9] M.G. Scherk, *Pen Pictures of Early Pioneer Life in Upper Canada* (Toronto: William Briggs, 1905), pp. 170, 171.

[10] Ball, p. 259.

[11] Jones, p. 76.

[12] Traill, pp. 124-25.

[13] Peter Russell, *Attitudes to Social Structure and Social Mobility in Upper Canada (1815-1840)*, PhD. Thesis, Carleton University, Ottawa, 1981, p. 78.

[14] Jones, p. 121.

[15] L.G. Reeds, *Agricultural Geography of Southern Ontario*, PhD. Thesis, University of Toronto, 1955, p. 131.

[16] J.J. Talman and Reverend M.A. Garland, "Pioneer Drinking Habits and the Rise of the Temperance Agitation in Upper Canada prior to 1840," in *Papers & Records*, Ontario Historical Society, Vol. 27 (1931), p. 341–64.

[17] G.P. de T. Glazerbrook, *Life in Ontario: A Social History* (Toronto: University of Toronto Press, 1968), p. 47.

[18] Phillip Dodds, *The Story of Agricultural Fairs and Exhibitions 1792-1967* (Picton: Picton Gazette Publishing, 1967), p. 12.

[19] J.J. Talman, "Agricultural Societies in Upper Canada," in *Papers & Records*, Ontario Historical Society, Vol. 27 (1931), p. 552.

[20] Jones, p. 163.

[21] Walter Riddell, "The Agricultural Society of Northumberland County," Riddell Papers, Archives of Ontario.

[22] Riddell, Riddell Papers.

[23] Johnson, p. 206.

[24] Johnson, p. 204.

[25] Publication of the Ontario Agricultural Hall of Fame. See also James Careless, *Union of the Canadas: The Growth of Canadian Institutions* (Toronto: McClelland and Stewart, 1967).

Women Cheesemakers and Their Craft

[1] Marjorie Cohen, *Women's Work, Markets and Economic Development in 19th-Century Ontario* (Toronto: University of Toronto Press, 1988), pp. 94, 96.

[2] Brenda Dyer, Sarah Kolasiewicz and Donna Stevenson, *Outstanding Women of Oxford County* (Woodstock: Oxford County Board of Education, 1979), pp. 13–20.

[3] James Crawford, "The Story of Canada's First Mammoth Cheese," The Crawford Papers, National Archives.

[4] Barb Fraser, "Empire Built on Butter," *Home and Country* (Winter, 1992), p. 7.

[5] Edward Moore, *When Cheese Was King: History of Cheese Factories in Oxford County* (Norwich: Norwich and District Historical Society, 1987), p. 42.

[6] Art Williams, *Woodstock Sentinel Review*, August 9, 1972. See also an account written by Peggy Graham from talk with local dairy farmer and resident expert on Lydia Ranney, Everitt Wilson. Both accounts are in the Cheese Factory Museum, Ingersoll, Ontario.

[7] Dyer, Kolasiewicz and Stevenson, p. 14; Williams.

[8] Harold A. Innis (ed.), *The Dairy Industry in Canada* (Toronto: Ryerson Press, 1937), p. 57.

[9] "Dairy Industry in Oxford County Indebted to Salford Pioneer." Undated, anonymous paper in Cheese Factory Museum, Ingersoll, Ontario.

[10] *Shenston's Gazeteer*, 1852.

[11] "Dairy Industry in Oxford County Indebted to Salford Pioneer."

[12] James Crawford, "The Story of Canada's First Mammoth Cheese," The Crawford Papers, National Archives, p. 7.

[13] Allan C. MacNeish, "Dairymen's Association of Western Ontario — A 100-year Odyssey of Dairy Progress," reprinted from *Canadian Dairy and Ice Cream Journal* (December 1966), p. 2.

[14] Fred Harrison, "Dairying and the Dairy Associations as Precursors of the Dairy Inspection Branch," *Dairy Branch and 100 Years of Service*, p. 28.

[15] Fraser, p. 7.

[16] See Cohen, Chapter 5. See also Jennifer Mueller, *Unravelling the Checkered Cloth: The Role of Upper Canadian Farm Women in the Market Economy: 1820–1860*, M.A. Thesis, Carleton University, 1992.

[17] Innis (ed.), pp. xvi, 60.

[18] Ewan Ross, "D.M. MacPherson — The Cheese King," in *Glengarry Life* (Alexandria: Glengarry Historical Society, 1976).

[19] James Ruddick, "The Cheese Industry," in Innis (ed.), p. 58.

[20] James Ruddick, Article on D.M. McPherson in *The Family Herald and Weekly Star*, January 28, 1931, McPherson Papers, University of Guelph.

The Cheese Poet of Oxford County

[1] William Arthur Deacon, *The Four Jameses* (Toronto: The Ryerson Press, 1953), p. 44.

[2] Pauline Greenhill, *True Poetry* (Montreal: McGill-Queens University Press, 1989), p. 8.

[3] Suzanne Zeller, *Inventing Canada: Early Victorian Science and the Idea of a Transcontinental Nation* (Toronto: University of Toronto Press, 1987), p. 6.

[4] Deacon, p. 49.

[5] James McIntyre, *Musings on the Banks of the Canadian Thames* (Stratford: Rowland Publishers, 1884), p. 21.

[6] McIntyre, p. 108.

[7] Deacon, p. 63.

8 John McCallum, *Unequal Beginnings: Agriculture and Economic Life in Quebec and Ontario until 1870* (Toronto: University of Toronto Press, 1980), p. 20.

9 Tonnu Tosine, *Cheese Factories in the Quinte-Upper St. Lawrence Area of Ontario 1865-1905*, Masters Thesis, York University, 1974, p. 35.

10 Agricultural Census, 1861, National Archives.

Harvey Farrington and Industrialization

1 Agricultural Census, 1851, 1861, National Archives.

2 Roger Hall and Gordon Dodds, *Picture History of Ontario* (Edmonton: Hurtig Publishers, 1978), p. 57.

3 Editorial, *Listowel Banner*, October 5, 1867.

4 Encyclopedia of Ontario.

5 "The Late Harvey Farrington," *The Husbandman*, March 12, 1879.

6 Moore, p. 60.

7 *Canada Farmer*, August 1, 1865.

8 *Canada Farmer*, November 1, 1864.

9 *Canada Farmer*, February 1, 1864, p. 22.

10 Moore, p. 73.

11 *Canada Farmer*, June 15, 1865, p. 182.

12 Jones, p. 265.

13 *Dairy and Ice Cream Journal*, 1964.

14 Moore, p. 60.

15 Jones, p. 255.

16 Carolyn Bart-Ridestra, *Cooperative and Scientific Dairying in Perth County*, Masters Essay, Wilfrid Laurier University, 1985, Stratford-Perth Archives, Stratford, Ontario.

17 *Canada Farmer*, June 15, 1865.

18 Jones, p. 257.

19 Earl Haslett, *The Growth and Decline of the Cheese Industry in Ontario 1864-1924* (Toronto: Economics Branch, Ontario Ministry of Agriculture and Food, 1978), p. 3.

20 *History of Balderson and Bathurst District*.

21 Haslett, *The Growth and Decline ...*, p. 3.

22 Haslett, *Factors in the Growth ...*, p. 22.

23 *Canada Farmer*, September 16, 1867, p. 278.

24 MacGillivray and Ross, pp. 46, 50.

25 Ruddick, "The Cheese Industry," p. 54.

26 Ross, p. 13.

27 Ruddick, "The Cheese Industry," pp. 55-56.

28 Bart-Ridestra, p. 10.

29 Haslett, *The Growth and Decline ...*, p. 9.

30 Joan Schwartz, "The Cherry Valley Cheese Making Co.," Unpublished Research Paper, National Archives.

31 McPherson Papers, University of Guelph.

Cheese Mammoths and Their Champions

1 Grant Miles, "1864 Cheese Meeting," April 21, 1977. Cheese Factory Museum.

2 Moore, p. 61.

3 *Canada Farmer*, August 1, 1865.

4 Moore, p. 61.

5 *Ingersoll Chronicle*, June 3, 1864.

6 Crawford, n.p.

7 Harry Whitwell, Personal Interview by Peggy Graham, 1977, Cheese Factory Museum.

8 Charles Chadwick, Letter to the Editor, *Ingersoll Chronicle*, August 10, 1866.

9 Byron Jenvey, Personal Interview by Peggy Graham, 1977, Cheese Factory Museum.

10 *Ingersoll Chronicle*, September 7, 1866.

11 Crawford, n.p.

12 Deacon, p. 60.

13 "The Mammoth Cheese," *Times Weekly*, Perth, September 20, 1962, p. 5.

[14] Anonymous, "The Big Cheese," 1893, MacPherson Family Papers, University of Guelph.

[15] Duncan MacPherson, Undated Letter (intended to correct the record on his father, D.M. MacPherson), MacPherson Family Papers.

[16] "The Mammoth Cheese," p. 5.

[17] Irvine, p. 123.

The Canadian Dairymen's Association

[1] Ambrose Keevil, *The Story of Fitch Lovell 1784-1970* (Chichester, England: Phillmore & Co., 1972), p. 3.

[2] Keevil, p. 13.

[3] Keevil, p. 35.

[4] *The Husbandman*, March 12, 1879.

[5] MacNeish, p. 6.

[6] Harrison, p. 28.

[7] *Canada Farmer*, April 15, 1867, p. 135.

[8] Bart-Ridestra, p. 25.

[9] Jim Baker, "Chronology of Dairying in Ontario," in *Dairy Branch and 100 Years of Service*, p. 212.

[10] Barta-Ridestra, p. 23.

[11] Baker, p. 217.

[12] Baker, p. 218.

[13] Bart-Ridestra, p. 24.

[14] Harrison, p. 29.

[15] Baker, p. 131.

[16] Innis (ed.), p. 59.

[17] Jardine, p. 60.

[18] Baker, p. 134.

[19] MacNeish, p. 6.

[20] Haslett, *The Growth and Decline* ..., p. 7.

[21] Johnston, pp. 550-51.

[22] *The Times Review*, Fort Erie, Ontario, April 26, 1972, p. 16.

[23] Haslett, *The Growth and Decline* ..., p. 8.

PART TWO:
"WHEN THE CHEESE MONEY PAID THE MORTGAGE"

Prologue

[1] Claude Flood, Personal Interview, Plum Hollow, Ontario, 1980. All subsequent quotations from Claude Flood in the text are from this interview.

[2] Talmage Stone, Personal Interview, Forfar, Ontario, 1980. All subsequent quotations from Talmage Stone in the text are from this interview.

[3] R.T. Naylor, *History of Canadian Business 1867-1914* (Toronto: James Lorimer and Co., 1975), Vol. I, pp. 104, 110.

[4] Hall and Dodds, p. 107.

[5] Haslett, *Factors in the Growth* ..., p. 126.

[6] Baker, p. 265.

[7] *An Economic Analysis of Cheesemaking in Ontario*, Ontario Ministry of Agriculture, 1933, Ontario Archives.

[8] Joseph Schull, *Ontario Since 1867* (Toronto: McClelland and Stewart, 1978), p. 70.

[9] E.P. Neufeld, *The Financial System of Canada, Its Growth and Development* (Toronto: MacMillan of Canada, 1972), p. 97.

[10] Naylor, Vol. I, p. 102.

[11] Schull, p. 187.

[12] Schull, p. 191.

[13] Margaret Evans, "Oliver Mowat: 19th-Century Ontario Liberal," in Donald Swainson (ed.), *Oliver Mowat's Ontario*. Papers presented to the Oliver Mowat Colloquium, Queen's University, November 1970, p. 43.

[14] Schull, p. 57.

[15] Haslett, *Factors in the Growth* ..., p. 45.

[16] Walter Riddell, "Hindrances to Progress in Canadian Agriculture with a View to their Removal," Riddell Family Papers, M.U. 2388, Box 1, Series A & B 1, Ontario Archives.

[17] Naylor, Vol. II, p. 177.

[18] Margaret Evens in Swainson (ed.), p. 78.

[19] Schull, p. 55.

[20] S.E.D. Shortt in Swainson (ed.), p. 216.

[21] Schull, p. 54.

[22] S.E.D. Shortt, p. 213.

[23] John D. Smart, *Patrons of Industry in Ontario*, M.A. Thesis, Carleton University, 1969, p. 67.

[24] Smart, pp. 37-40.

[25] See E.C. Drury, *Farmer Premier: Memoirs of the Honorable E.C. Drury* (Toronto: McClelland and Stewart, 1966).

[26] Haslett, *The Growth and Decline ...*, p. 8.

A Day at the Cheese Factory

[1] John Fraser, Personal Interview, Vankleek Hill, Ontario, 1980. All subsequent quotations from John Fraser in the text are from this interview.

[2] Steve and Joan Robinson, Personal Interview, Almonte, Ontario, 1992.

[3] Jim Baker, Personal Interview, Guelph, Ontario, 1992. All subsequent quotations from Jim Baker in the text are from this interview.

[4] D.M. Irvine, *Cheddar Cheese Manufacture* (Toronto: Ontario Ministry of Agriculture and Food), p. 13. Much of the technical detail on cheesemaking here is drawn from this manual, supplemented with information supplied in a personal interview with Dr. Arthur Hill, University of Guelph, 1992.

[5] Fred Day, Personal Interview, Listowel, Ontario, 1992. All subsequent quotations from Fred Day in the text are from this interview.

[6] Irvine, p. 15.

[7] Doug Rowe, Personal Interview, Warkworth, Ontario, 1981. All subsequent quotations from Doug Rowe in the text are from this interview.

[8] Gordon Henry, Personal Interview, Ingersoll, Ontario, 1981. All subsequent quotations from Gordon Henry in the text are from this interview.

[9] Irvine, p. 24.

[10] Glen Martin, Personal Interview, Ripley, Ontario, 1981. All subsequent quotations from Glen Martin in the text are from this interview.

[11] Harold Kingston, Personal Interview, Harrowsmith, Ontario, 1981. All subsequent quotations from Harold Kingston in the text are from this interview.

[12] Irvine, p. 17.

Claude Flood's Culture

[1] Jack Beaton, Personal Interview, Ontario, 1992.

[2] Frank Robinson, Personal Interview, Kemptville, Ontario, 1982. Robinson was the head of cheese instruction at the Kemptville Dairy School.

[3] Lloyd Stacey, Personal Interview, Forfar, Ontario, 1992.

[4] Hereward Senior, in Swainson (ed.), p. 139.

[5] *Women of Canada* (Ottawa: National Council of Women, 1898), p. 127.

Sanitation and Cheese Factory Inspectors

[1] Jack Bain, Personal Interview, London, Ontario, 1980, 1981. All subsequent quotations from Jack Bain in the text are from this interview.

[2] Jardine, pp. 60, 61.

[3] Jardine, p. 66.

[4] See *An Economic Analysis of Cheese Factory Operations in Ontario*, Ontario Department of Agriculture, 1933. Many of the cheesemakers I interviewed for this book had no more than grade 8 education, some had less.

[5] Haslett, *Factors in the Growth ...*, pp. 62, 79.

[6] Baker, p. 151.

[7] Baker, p. 65.

[8] Baker, p. 242.

[9] Jim Baker, Personal Interview, Guelph, Ontario, 1981.

"Missionary Work"

[1] Harrison, p. 30.

[2] Russ Martin, Personal Interview, Dorchester, Ontario, 1981. All subsequent quotations from Russ Martin in the text are from this interview.

Cheese Boards and Market Control

[1] Baker, p. 199.

[2] Baker, p. 286.

[3] James Ruddick, Bulletin from Dairy and Cold Storage Commission, Department of Agriculture, Ottawa, Ontario, 1915.

[4] Baker, p. 351.

[5] "History of Cheesemaking in Ontario," Address to Annual Meeting of Western Ontario Cheesemakers' Association, OAC, Guelph, March 12, 1964, Ministry of Agriculture Records, Ontario Archives.

[6] Haslett, *Factors in the Growth* ..., p. 31.

[7] Innis (ed.), pp. 159-61.

[8] Innis (ed.), p. 164.

[9] Innis (ed.), p. 159.

[10] Jones, p. 259.

[11] Baker, p. 266.

[12] Innis (ed.), p. 163

[13] Baker, p. 270.

[14] Baker, p. 291.

[15] Haslett, *The Growth and Decline* ..., p. 17.

[16] Ina Arnold (Hector Arnold's widow), Personal Interview, Campbellford, Ontario, 1981.

[17] Thomas Wells, *Royal Commission on Milk*, 1947, Dairy Branch Files, Ontario Archives.

[18] Innis (ed.), pp. 140, 153, 155.

[19] Baker, p. 284.

[20] Haslett, *The Growth and Decline* ..., p. 18.

[21] Haslett, *Factors in the Growth* ..., pp. 124, 126.

[22] Ontario Dairy Products Manufacturers' Files, 1939, Ministry of Agriculture and Food Records, Ontario Archives.

[23] Baker, pp. 282, 286, 293.

[24] Jim Baker, Personal Interview, Guelph, Ontario, 1980.

[25] Haslett, *The Growth and Decline* ..., p. 15.

[26] Baker, pp. 262, 268.

[27] Haslett, *Factors in the Growth* ..., p. 74.

Money and the Board of Directors

[1] *An Economic Analysis of Cheesemaking in Ontario*, 1933.

[2] Baker, p. 251.

The Master Craftsmen

[1] This is supported by Michael Bliss, *A Canadian Millionaire: The Life and Business Times of Sir Joseph Flavelle* (Toronto: MacMillan of Canada, 1978), p. 237.

[2] Lane and Fox, p. 18.

[3] Baker, p. 290.

PART THREE: DECLINE AND NEGLECT

Prologue

[1] Robert Bothwell, Ian Drummond, and John English, *Canada Since 1945: Power, Politics and Provincialism* (Toronto: University of Toronto Press, 1981), p. 63.

[2] Donald Creighton, *The Forked Road: Canada 1939-1957* (Toronto: McClelland and Stewart, 1976), p. 116.

[3] Bothwell, p. 71.

[4] Schull, p. 318.

[5] Bothwell, p. 100.

[6] Creighton, pp. 78, 89, 222.

[7] Creighton, pp. 118-119.

[8] Schull, pp. 324, 328.

[9] Creighton, pp. 80-81.

10 Bothwell, p. 265.

11 Creighton, pp. 56-57.

12 Creighton, p. 257.

13 Bothwell, p. 203.

14 Creighton, p. 259.

15 Bothwell, p. 184.

16 Baker, p. 304.

17 Wells, p. 124.

18 Schull, p. 337.

19 Enid Macdonald, Personal Interview, Alexandria, Ontario, 1980.

20 Schull, p. 337.

21 Schull, pp. 334, 345, 353.

22 Henry F. Noble, "Trends in Farm Abandonment," *Canadian Journal of Agricultural Economics*, Vol. 10, No. 1 (1962), pp. 69, 72, 73.

23 Schull, pp. 315-16.

24 Schull, p. 334.

25 Haslett, *Cheddar Cheese Factories in Ontario*, Ontario Ministry of Agriculture, Farm Economics Branch, 1965, pp. 14-15.

26 Fraser, Personal Interview.

27 Haslett, *Cheddar Cheese Factories*, p. 38.

28 Bothwell, p. 230.

29 Schull, p. 379

Brought to You by . . . the Makers of Processed Cheese

1 Kraft Foods Company Memo. Subject: Canadian Company. ACFK 6232, 500 Peshtigo Court, Chicago, Illinois.

2 *The Kraft Story*, (Chicago: Kraft Foods, n.d.), p. 7.

3 Tom Quinn, Personal Interview, Montreal, Quebec, 1982; Letter from G.W. Bland, V.P. Marketing, Kraft Foods, to Heather Menzies, January 23, 1983.

4 John Warnock, *Profit Hungry* (Vancouver: New Star Books, 1978), p. 102.

5 Baker, p. 286.

6 *Shenston's Gazeteer*, p. 45.

7 Moore, p. 83.

8 *Shenston's Gazeteer*, p. 45.

9 Innis (ed.), p. 65.

10 Wendy Herman, "An Empire Started Here," *The Times Review*, Fort Erie, April 26, 1972.

11 John Beaton, in *Dairy Branch and 100 Years of Service*, p. 40.

12 Baker, p. 268.

13 Herman.

14 *The Kraft Story*, p. 7.

15 Bain, p. 23.

A Blow to the British Connection

1 Wells, pp. 124-25; Sam Ault, Personal Interview, Place, Date. All subsequent quotations from Sam Ault in the text are from this interview.

2 Haslett, *Cheddar Cheese Factories*, p. 113.

3 Annual Reports, Ontario Ministry of Agriculture, 1952, 1953.

4 Lane and Fox, p. 25.

5 Baker, Personal Interview, 1981.

Forced March to Modern Times

1 Baker, Personal Interview, 1981.

2 Dairy Commissioner's Files, Ministry of Agriculture Records, RG 16-169, Box 8, Ontario Archives.

3 Albert Ouellette, Personal Interview, Montreal, Quebec, 1980.

4 Dairy Commissioner's Files.

5 Everett Biggs, Personal Interview, Pembroke, Ontario, 1983. All subsequent quotations from Everett Biggs in the text are from this interview, unless otherwise noted.

6 Gerald Ackerman, Personal Interview, Picton, Ontario, 1980.

7 Bob Carbert, 1973, Memo to Jack Palmer, Milk Industry Branch, Ontario Ministry of Agriculture and Food, Dairy Commissioner's files, correspondence.

8 Haslett, *Cheddar Cheese Factories*, p. 14.

9 Bain, *Report* p. 28.

George McLaughlin's Marketing Board

1 Jim Jewson, "Development of an Open and Representative Policy-Making Approach to the Dairy Industry by Government," in *Dairy Branch and 100 Years of Service*, p. 78.

2 Jewson, pp. 83, 85.

3 Everett Biggs, *The Challenge of Achievement: The Ontario Milk Marketing Board's First 25 Years of Operation: 1965-1990* (Mississauga: Ontario Milk Marketing Board, 1990), p. 18.

4 Biggs, p. 25.

5 Baker, Personal Interview, 1981.

6 Biggs, pp. 33, 35.

7 Biggs, pp. 34, 35.

8 S.G. Hennessey, *Report of the Ontario Milk Industry Inquiry Committee*, (Toronto: Government of Ontario, 1965), p. 147.

9 Hennessey, p. 97.

10 Hennessey, pp. 103-105.

11 Hennessey, p. 97.

12 Hennessey, p. 106.

13 Hennessey, p. 104.

14 Hennessey, pp. 271-72.

15 Biggs, p. 9.

16 See Biggs, pp. 31, 38, 108.

17 Hennessey, p. 156.

18 Hennessey, p. 44.

19 Peter Lewington, *Canada's Holsteins* (Toronto: Fitzhenry and Whiteside, 1983), p. 105.

20 George McLaughlin, Personal Interview, Beaverton, Ontario, 1981. All subsequent quotations from George McLaughlin in the text are from this interview, unless otherwise noted.

21 Warnock, p. 102.

22 Lane and Fox, p. 55.

23 Biggs, p. 96.

24 Lane and Fox, pp. 49-50.

Shutting Down Hector Arnold

1 Lorne Hurd, Personal Interview, Toronto, Ontario, 1981.

2 Biggs, p. 65.

3 George Wood, Personal Interview, Ivanhoe, Ontario, 1982.

4 Biggs, p. 41. The words are attributed to Agriculture Minister Bill Stewart.

5 Biggs, p. 109.

The Closing Out Program

1 Bain, p. 28.

2 Bain, p. 30. Hennessey, p. 90, did suggest that there was a place for small, craft-scale factories making traditional cheddar cheese.

3 Bain, pp. 23-25.

4 Haslett, *Cheddar Cheese Factories*, pp. 25, 27, 32, 36, 37.

5 Bain, p. 10.

6 Bain, pp. 4, 6.

7 Baker, Personal Interview, 1992.

8 M.T. Murchie and M.H. Stewart, *Report to the Milk Commission of Ontario on Industrial Milk Processing Industry*, Dairy Commissioner's Files, 1969, Ontario Archives.

9 Murchie and Stewart, p. 17.

10 Barry Haggett, Personal Interview, Plum Hollow, Ontario, 1983. All subsequent quotations from Barry Haggett in the text are from this interview, unless otherwise noted.

11 Jean F. Poirier, "The Outlook for Small Cheese Factories in Ontario," Honours Paper for B.E.S., Geography, University of Waterloo, 1972, p. 11.

12 David George, Finance and Administration Branch, Ontario Ministry of Agriculture and Food, Letter to Heather Menzies, February 25, 1992.

The Kraft Boycott

1 Bothwell, p. 279.

2 Kari Levitt, *Silent Surrender* (Toronto: MacMillan of Canada, 1970), p. 62.

3 Warnock, p. 103.

4 Warnock, p. 96. See also Don Mitchell, *The Politics of Food* (Toronto: James Lorimer & Co., 1975), p. 133.

5 Warnock, pp. 95-96.

6 George Grant, *Technology and Empire* (Toronto: House of Anansi, 1969), p. 138.

7 Lane and Fox, p. 48.

8 Biggs, p. 108.

9 Raymond Niblock, Correspondence, July 29, 1971, Dairy Commissioner's Files, Ontario Archives.

10 Biggs, p. 109.

11 Biggs, p. 89.

12 Fred Gudmundson, Telephone Interview, Winnipeg, Manitoba, 1981.

13 *Ottawa Citizen*, February 23, 1973.

14 Warnock, p. 101.

15 Biggs, p. 115.

16 Biggs, p. 114.

17 Jean Chamberland, Personal Interview, Plantagenet, Ontario, 1983.

What Price Heritage?

1 Lane and Fox, p. 70.

2 Bob Rowe, Personal Interview, Warkworth, Ontario, 1982.

3 David Lees and James Lawrence, "Red Tape Does Not a Cheddar Make," *Harrowsmith*, Vol. 3, No. 3, p. 43.

4 Bruce Kingston, Personal Interview, Harrowsmith, Ontario, 1982.

AFTERWORD

1 William Morris, Art and Society: Lectures and Essays by William Morris (Boston: George's Hill Publications, 1993), p. 21.
2 Harold MacKenzie, Head, Cheese Grading and Inspection, S.W. Ontario, Ontario Ministry of Food and Agriculture, Telephone Interview, 1994. All subsequent quotations from Harold MacKenzie in the text are from this interview.

3 "Fact Sheet on Listeria Monocytogenes," Department of Food Science, University of Guelph.

4 Jack Richardson, President of the Cooperative, Telephone Interview, 1994.

5 Howard French, Telephone Interview, 1994.

Photo Credits

❦

Front Cover: Courtesy of Ingersoll Cheese Factory Museum, Ingersoll, Ontario.

p. 3:   Courtesy of Ingersoll Cheese Factory Museum.

p. 7:   Courtesy of Stratford-Perth Archives, Stratford, Ontario.

p. 10:   Courtesy of Carol Graham Baxter.

p. 13:   From Edward Moore, *When Cheese Was King: A History of Cheese Factories in Oxford County* (Norwich: Norwich and District Historical Society, 1987).

p. 17:   *Top:* Frontispiece from Mrs. C.P. Traill, *The Canadian Emmigrant Housekeeper's Guide* (Toronto: Lovell & Gibson, 1862).
Bottom: Courtesy of Stratford-Perth Archives.

p. 21:   From Thad. W. Leavitt, *History of Leeds and Grenville, Ontario, from 1749 to 1879* (Brockville: Recorder Press, 1879).

p. 28:   Courtesy of the Norwich Township Archives, Norwich, Ontario.

p. 30:   Adapted from Brenda Dyer, Sarah Kolasiewicz and Donna Stevenson, *Outstanding Women of Oxford County* (Woodstock: Oxford County Board of Education, 1979).

p. 33:   From William Arthur Deacon, *The Four Jameses* (Toronto: The Ryerson Press, 1953).

p. 37:   *Top:* Courtesy of the Ontario Agricultural Hall of Fame.
Bottom: From *Canadian Dairy and Ice Cream Journal,* December 1966.

p. 38:   From *When Cheese Was King.*

p. 41:   Courtesy of Archieval Collection, University of Guelph Library.

p. 42:   Courtesy of National Archives of Canada.

p. 45:   From Iona Joy, *Cheese Factories of Rideau Township* (North Gower: Rideau Township Historical Society, 1990).

p. 47:   From *Dairy Branch and 100 Years of Service* (Toronto: Ontario Ministry of Agriculture and Food, 1988).

p. 48:   From *Dairy Branch.*

p. 49:   *Top:* Courtesy of Ingersoll Cheese Factory Museum.
Bottom: Archival Collections University of Guelph Library.

p. 55: *Top:* Courtesy of Stratford-Perth Archives, Stratford, Ontario.
Bottom: From *Canadian Dairy and Ice Cream Journal*, December 1966.

p. 57: From *When Cheese Was King.*

p. 59: *Top Left:* Courtesy of National Archives of Canada.
Top Right: Courtesy of Stratford-Perth Archives.
Bottom: From *Dairy Branch.*

p. 61: Courtesy of National Archives of Canada.

p. 76: *Top:* From *Harrowsmith Magazine*, No. 15.
Bottom: Courtesy of Forfar Dairy.

p. 67: *From When Cheese Was King.*

p. 71: Courtesy of Heather Menzies.

p. 74: *Top Left & Right:* Courtesy of Heather Menzies.
Bottom: Courtesy of Stratford-Perth Archives.

p. 64: From *Dairy Branch.*

p. 79: From *Harrowsmith Magazine*, No. 15
p. 81: *Top:* Courtesy of Jack Bain.
Bottom: From *Dairy Branch.*

p. 84: *Top:* Courtesy of Harold Kingston.
Bottom: Courtesy of Stratford-Perth Archives.

p. 90: *Top:* From *Harrowsmith Magazine*, No. 15.
Bottom: From *When Cheese Was King.*

p. 93 : *Top Left & Bottom:* Courtesy of Stratford-Perth Archives, Listowel and Area Division, Listowel, Ontario.
Top Right: Courtesy of Harold Kingston.

p. 97: Courtesy of Fred and Edith Day.

p. 98: From *Dairy Branch.*

p. 99 From *Dairy Branch.*

p. 103: From *When Cheese Was King.*

p. 110: *Top:* Courtesy of Heather Menzies.
Bottom: From *When Cheese Was King.*

p. 114: Courtesy of Doug and Emma Rowe.

p. 119: *Top Left & Bottom:* From Everett Biggs, *The Challenge of Achievement: The Ontario Milk Marketing Board's First 25 Years of Operation, 1965 to 1990* (Mississauga: The Ontario Milk Marketing Board, 1990).
Top Right: From Gerald Ackerman, *History of Cheesemaking in Prince Edward County* (Picton: The Picton Gazette Publishing Co., 1971).

p. 121: *Top:* From *History of Cheesemaking in Prince Edward County.*
Bottom: Courtesy of Black River Cheese Co. Ltd.

p. 124: Courtesy of Harold Kingston.

p. 127: Courtesy of Sam Ault.

p. 128: Courtesy of Sam Ault.

p. 138: Courtesy of Fred Day.

p. 139: From *When Cheese Was King.*

p. 144: From *Union Farmer*, September 1971, courtesy of Heather Menzies.

p. 153: *Top:* Courtesy of Eldorado Cheese Limited.
Bottom: Courtesy of Empire Cheese & Butter Co-op.

p. 155: *Top:* Courtesy of Pine River Cheese & Butter Co-operative.
Bottom: Courtesy of Michael Dawber.

p. 159: From *Canadian Dairy and Ice Cream Journal*, December 1966.

p. 164: Courtesy of Blanshard & Nissouri Cheese & Butter Co. Ltd.

p. 165: Courtesy of Ingersoll Museums, Ingersoll, Ontario.

Acknowledgements

This book has been over ten years in the making, and derives from the generous support of many. First and foremost, the grand old men — and women — of the cheese business whose voices and stories form the backbone of this book: Jack Bain, Fred and Edith Day, Claude Flood, Talmage, Ross and Marion Stone, Wes and Ken Krotz, Russ Martin, Doug, Bob and Emma Rowe, Harold, Bruce and Hazel Kingston, John and Pauline Fraser, Glen Martin, Sam Ault, Gerald Ackerman, Albert Oullette, Jean Chamberland, Ina Arnold, Harold Douglas, Howard Stacey, George Wood and Barry Haggett.

There are others in government, business, and the farming community who graciously talked to me as well: Jim Baker, Everett Biggs, George McLaughlin, Tom Quinn, Walter Miller, Fred Gudmundson, Art Hill, Donald Irvine, Frank Robinson, Owen Irwin, Jack Beaton, Earl Haslett, Stephen Beckley, Bob Jardine, Lorne Hurd, Arnold Johnston, Gordon Henry, Frank Leslie, Joan Leslie Chase, Marion Hale, Phyllis Facey Sutherland, Mac Hicks, Gene Keogh, and Enid Macdonald.

There are also numerous fine academics who contributed valuable advice along the way: Keith Johnson, Alison Prentice, Julian Gwyn, Douglas McCalla, Stephen Rodd, J.J. Talman. Also, archivists, including Catherine Shepard, Nancy Sadek, Shirley Lovell, James Anderson, Carolyn Bart-Ridestra and Lutzen Ridestra, Margaret Ellison, and Lisa Miettinen.

There were many, many others who have lent me photographs or given me extra information. Some of these include Pauline Fraser, Carol (Graham) Baxter, Muriel Code, Mrs. Tamblyn, and Joan and Steve Robinson. I also wish to gratefully acknowledge the important financial support of the Canada Council.

And finally, I wish to thank my friends and family for their support and unflagging encouragement, including my mother Anne, my partner Miles, and my son, Donald. As for all the supportive friends, well, there's Pat and Jan, Chris and Joan and Jen, and more. *Thanks everyone.*